Great Ideas

for

Gift Baskets, Bags, & Boxes

Kathy Lamancusa, C.P.D., R.M.C.

TAB Books

Division of McGraw-Hill, Inc.

New York   San Francisco   Washington, D.C.   Auckland   Bogotá
Caracas   Lisbon   London   Madrid   Mexico City   Milan
Montreal   New Delhi   San Juan   Singapore
Sydney   Tokyo   Toronto

Notices

Design Master color tool®	Colorado Dye and Chemical
Creatively Yours™	Loctite Corporation
Sahara®	Smithers-Oasis
Oasis®	
Mini Deco®	
Styrofoam®	Dow Chemical

© 1992 by **TAB Books.**
TAB Books is a division of McGraw-Hill, Inc.

pbk   8 9 10 11 12 13 14 15 DOC/DOC 9 9 8 7 6 5

Library of Congress Cataloging-in-Publication Data

Lamancusa, Kathy.
   Great ideas for gift baskets, bags, and boxes / by Kathy
Lamancusa.
     p.   cm.
   Includes index.
   ISBN 0-8306-4035-5 (pbk.)
   1. Handicraft. 2. Baskets. 3. Gifts. I. Title.
TT157.L22   1992
745.594—dc20   92-18421
                                  CIP

Acquisitions Editor: Stacy Varavvas-Pomeroy
Book Editor: April D. Nolan
Director of Production: Katherine G. Brown
Book Design: Joanne M. Slike
Cover Photograph: Thompson Photography, Baltimore, MD
Cover Design: Lori E. Schlosser
Color photography: Studio 7, Canton, OH
Black and white photography: Visual Design Concepts,
   North Canton, Oh.
Line Illustrations: Wagaman Creative Graphics, Hanover, Pa.

CHD
3899

Contents

Chapter 1
Starting Out

Chapter 2
Ribbons and Bows

Chapter 3
Special Occasions

Chapter 4
Romantic Designs

Chapter 5
Holiday Designs

Chapter 6
Wine and Food Designs

Chapter 7
Bed and Bath Designs

Chapter 8
All Through the House

Chapter 9
Children's Designs

To my husband, Joe

Thank you for your constant support and guidance through all of our new opportunities and endeavors. Looking forward to the days when we can just "grow old together" . . . enjoying the fruits of our labors and excitedly watching our boys grow into men with families of their own—thanking God that we can be a part of it all!

❧ Acknowledgments ❧

A special thank you to:

The Kathy Lamancusa in-house design team who created, designed, edited, photographed and helped in every step of the production of *Gift Baskets, Bags & Boxes:*

Katherine Lamancusa
Mary Annette Salpietra

❧ Suppliers ❧

Thank you to the following suppliers who provided materials for this book:

AMERICAN OAK PRESERVING CO.
601 Mulberry St.
North Judson, IN 46366

B.B. WORLD CORP.
2200 So. Maple Ave.
Los Angeles, CA 90011

CARNIVAL ARTS
P.O. Box 4145
Northbrook, IL 60065

C.M. OFFRAY & SON INC.
Route 24 Box 601
Chester, NJ 07903

DESIGN MASTER COLOR TOOL, INC.
P.O. Box 601
Boulder, CO 80306

FALK INDUSTRIES
155 Spring St.
New York, NY 10012

LION RIBBON COMPANY
100 Metro Way
Secaucus, NJ 07096

LOCTITE CORP.
4450 Cranwood Court
Cleveland, OH 44128

MCGINLEY MILLS
P.O. Box 68
Phillipsburg, NJ 08865

RELIANCE TRADING CORP.
3716 S. Iron St.
Chicago, IL 60609

SMITHERS-OASIS CORP.
919 Marvin Ave.
Kent, OH 44240

ZUCKER FEATHER PRODUCTS
512 North East St.
California, MO 65018

❧Introduction❧

The giving of gifts is part of our heritage. We want to please our friends and family with the gifts we select for the special times in their lives: birthdays, anniversaries, the birth of a new baby, and the time when they are "over the hill" to name but a few. We certainly can't forget special holidays such as Christmas, Halloween and Valentine's Day.

Gifts also express special feelings for the romantic occasions in our lives, such as weddings, showers, and even more intimate times shared between two people.

Children love to give and receive gifts, as well. What can surpass the joy and anticipation in the eyes of children as they prepare a special gift for a special person?

It is for all the above reasons that this book was written. Giving is a special time, and this book will help you make your gift giving occasion more unique and memorable. I love to prepare special wrappings in which to enclose my chosen gifts. If these special wrappings are in the form of a gift basket, bag, or box, often the wrapping becomes a second gift and is remembered for a long time after it is given.

I've classified each project as: *beginner, intermediate,* or *advanced,* but these levels are not ones of difficulty. In fact, this book was designed so that anyone could pick it up and complete any project within its pages.

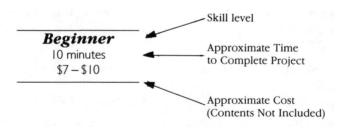

The beginner projects are designed to be quick and extremely simple: Even a child could read and follow these instructions. The intermediate designs are a bit more elaborate in the means of construction, requiring more steps to complete the designs. The advanced designs are lengthy in their construction process and require a wide variety of materials. Nonetheless, with a little concentration, even a novice designer should be able to complete all the projects that have intermediate and advanced classifications.

Approximate lengths of time are given for each of the designs, but keep in mind that these are estimations based on the average time of construction. If you are a novice in design, it might take you a few minutes longer, while if you are a veteran, you might find that you can complete the projects in half the time listed.

For each of the projects, you'll also find a price range listed. Use it as a guide in understanding how much your project will cost to make. (The approximate cost given is based only on the materials required to complete the project; it does not include anything you might want to put in your gift basket, box, or bag.)

Remember that a wide variety of price ranges exist—based on areas of the country as well as on the quality and construction of the item you are purchasing. For example, a stem of daisies can cost 59¢ in one store and $4.99 in another. The difference in the product will probably be great, all the way from type of fabric used for the flower (cheap or good-quality) to the kind of stem it has (plastic or hand-wrapped). Keep this in mind as you purchase items for your projects and compare them with the listed price ranges.

Chapter 1 will explain all the tools and supplies you'll need to get started in creating your own baskets, bags, and boxes. A brief overview of the steps necessary for construction of any one of the containers is included, as is a special section on balloons—what to know and how to include them in your designs.

Bow making and basic ribbon techniques are explained, step by step, in chapter 2. You'll learn to create a basic bow, a tailored bow, and an embellished bow. Instructions are given for making ribbon fans and loops and for braiding ribbon. This chapter also includes a variety of tips and techniques helpful when creating ribbon embellishments.

The designs begin in chapter 3. The projects contained in this book are designed as idea starters for you. You can create a project exactly like what you see in the book, but you'll learn enough tips and techniques to adapt and change the designs to fit your needs.

Chapter 3 shows a variety of designs for special occasions. Included in this chapter you'll find baskets, boxes, and bags for birthdays, thank-you gifts, bon voyage parties, patriotic occasions, "over the hill" friends, and new babies. Anniversaries are a popular gift-giving time, so I've included a design for that occasion, too. Just for fun, I've thrown in a "Duffer's Gift Bag" for the golfer in your life.

Romantic designs are the theme of chapter 4, with a wide variety of projects geared to weddings and showers. Keep in mind, however, that many of these designs would be perfect for including in an intimate evening party, decorating a Victorian home, or giving to a friend who is a romantic at heart. A unique grouping of wedding projects doubles as table centerpieces and attendants gifts. One more twist to this grouping is that the floral embellishments can also be used as hair adornments for the bridesmaids on the day of the wedding!

Holidays are our most popular gift-giving times. I've made sure you had a lot to work with in chapter 5 for a wide variety of holidays. Christmas and Halloween top off the list of designs, but other holidays represented include: Valentine's Day, St. Patrick's Day, Mother's Day, and the coming of spring and Easter.

I've found that gift baskets filled with wine and specialty foods are one of the most popular areas of gift-basket giving. In chapter 6, you'll find such projects for a variety of occasions—from corporate giving all the way to special baskets to bring to a friend's house when you visit for an evening of card- or game-playing.

Decorative treatments for wine bottles are also included in chapter 6. These were designed to be created in a minimal amount of time—perfect for the last-minute gift as you run out of the house.

Chapter 7 deals with designs for the bedroom and bathroom. You'll find baskets filled with soaps, towels, and many other personal items. One of the designs here was created especially for a little girl and another for an intimate evening with a loved one. Potpourri is often used as a decorative accent to bedrooms because of its beautiful texture and wonderful aromas. Some of the baskets in this chapter use potpourri as an accent.

All Through the House is the title of chapter 8. The designs in this chapter are useful for a variety of locations around the home. Some of the designs could hang on the wall, others can be placed on the hearth, and still others will find their home in the kitchen. Whatever the room you need to decorate with bags, boxes, or baskets, this chapter will get your creative juices flowing.

Chapter 9 has a variety of designs for children to make as well as to receive. The projects in this chapter are very easy and fast to create, and most are of minimal cost. Because clowns are a favorite of children, I've designed a box that looks just like a smiling, happy clown face. Stickers and paints are two of the items often used in this chapter.

I hope these designs will get you started on the road to creating many baskets, bags, and boxes as gifts for friends and family. Watch the products displayed in craft, floral, and gift shops—the market is always introducing new and exciting products to use.

If you have any questions or would like to share some new ideas with me, please write to me at TAB Books. I'd love to hear from you!

Starting Out

You are entering a wonderful world of gift-giving and special-occasion design. Allow your imagination to take hold as you learn all the basic information necessary to create spectacular gift baskets, bags, and boxes. Then try several of the designs I give later in the book, and you'll soon be ready to design your own marvelous creations for any occasion or event.

TOOLS & SUPPLIES

A great deal of time and effort can be saved by simply having the right supplies. Let's discuss each of the tools and supplies that are important.

Scissors and wire cutters. A good set of wire cutters is extremely important. Invest in a pair that is top-quality, and they will last a long time. Wire cutters are used to cut any materials that are wire or have wire cores. Choose a pair of scissors that is comfortable in your hand. Scissors are used to cut ribbons and other non-wire items. Never attempt to cut wire with your good scissors; the blades will get nicked and scratched, and, in a short time, will no longer cut ribbon.

Ruler or tape measure. The ruler or tape measure is used to accurately determine the width and height of a design, as well as to assist in determining proper flower-stem length.

Floral tape. Floral tape is a nonsticky tape available in green, white, brown, and other colors. It is used to wrap stems of flowers and create bunches of dried and silk floral materials before attaching these bunches to a project.

ADHESIVES & GLUES

A wide variety of adhesives is available in the market today. When you choose one, be need-specific: Know what you want to glue together, then choose the glue that will do the job. Here are some specifics about product categories that should assist you in your decision making process.

Look for the Creatively Yours line of adhesives at your local craft or floral shop. It is the most complete line of products that fits all gift-basket decorating needs.

Hot glue guns and glue sticks. Glue guns are indispensable to designers. When proper care is taken, they are fast and easy to use and offer superior bonding on a number of surfaces.

Glue guns use shaped glue sticks, which are a mixture of plastics, resins, and adhesives. These are inserted into the back of the gun and pass through a heating chamber that melts and activates the glue. The glue gun extrudes quantities of glue that have been melted to a temperature of 350° F. Because of the temperature of the glue, this product should be kept away from children.

Newer, lower-temperature glue guns are on the market and could be considered for younger hands. However, at times, the glue that comes out of these guns is not as strong as the glue used with the high-temperature guns.

Hot-melt adhesives form a secure bond within 30–90 seconds following application. Most hot-melt adhesives will be affected by temperature and weather changes (they could melt in higher temperatures and crack in extreme cold), so exercise caution when using them outdoors for extended periods of time.

Crafter's Cement. This brand of adhesive is an ideal alternative to white glue. It is a slow-set adhesive, which allows the designer to be creative and alter pieces as the design is being created; however is not runny or "drippy" like traditional white glue. In addition, it is not affected by temperature changes and is perfect for attaching flowers and ribbons.

Clear silicones. Silicone should be the product of choice when you want to add depth to dimensional projects. Its ability to bridge gaps and ridges makes it perfect for porous substances such as fabrics, flowers, and styrene foam. Clear silicones are also waterproof, as well as being an excellent outdoor adhesive.

Project Plus. This two-part brand-name adhesive provides a bond that resists moisture and solvents. It works best on hard-to-bond items such as metals, plastics, and glass.

Super Glues. Considered instant adhesives, Super Glues work very well on wood and are great for attaching beads, jewels, flowers, and other embellishments. Super Glues are available in gel formulas that bond to more surfaces and work faster. You can also get glue pens with pin-point accuracy tips.

FASTENERS

U-shaped pins. You might hear several different names for this type of pin, including: pole pins, greening pins, craft pins, and so on. They are used to attach moss onto foam and to attach materials to wreaths or floral designs created in or on gift baskets.

Corsage pins. These are used to attach ribbons or other similar materials to foams, wreaths, baskets, bags, or boxes. Because of their large, decorative pin heads, they are used when they will be seen for decorative purposes. Corsage pins are also inserted into corsages, which should be attached to a design in a way that they can be removed and worn.

Straight pins. The common straight pin is an invaluable item with hundreds of uses. These pins are available in many lengths, as well as with various sizes of pin heads. Decide what is best for you by the materials you will be working with.

Wire. You can purchase wire in its natural color or painted green. Green-painted wire is usually more costly and most often will end up being floral taped, so there is no great need to purchase green over natural.

Wire is also available in a number of diameters or gauges. The larger the gauge, the thinner the wire will be. For example, 30 gauge (ga.) wire is much thinner than 16 gauge (ga.) wire. Usually used to lengthen flower stems, 20-gauge wire will also help support softer drieds or flowers. Thinner wires can be used to secure, support, or attach items to gift baskets.

Cloth-covered wire is a very thin wire that has been covered with cloth threads. It is often used to secure bows. The cloth covering makes the bow secure without bare wire slipping and releasing the loops of the bow. Cloth-covered wire is also useful to attach items or clusters to bags, boxes, or baskets.

Chenille stem. Commonly known as pipe cleaners, these are useful for securing bows and can be inserted into foams. These stems are wires twisted with tiny chenille fibers. They are also useful for attaching items or clusters; however, they are usually more visible and are not used as often as cloth-covered wire. Cloth-covered wire is also less expensive than chenille stems to use.

Wooden picks. A wooden pick has one blunt end and one pointed end. A wire is attached to the blunt end and is used to wrap around items secured to the pick. The pointed end is used to insert materials into the design. Wooden picks can be used to form ribbon loops, create a firm stem for a cluster of dried materials and also lengthen silk flower stems.

To attach a wood pick, lay the wired end of the pick against the item, overlapping at least 1/2 inch (1.3 cm). Wrap the wire securely around the item and pick a few times, then down around the stems *only* a few times, and then back up and around the item and wood pick again. This will help eliminate the item from twisting and turning on the wood pick.

FLORAL FOAMS

When using florals in your gift containers, your choice of foam is very important to the finished design. Each type of arranging foam is designed to suit a particular need. Because of the various compositions of each foam, each type must be attached to its container in a different manner.

Silk and dried foam. For any type of dried or silk materials you want to incorporate into a design, you should use the floral foam made specifically for that purpose (such as Sahara brand). This type of foam is softer, so you need not reinforce dried stems with wire before inserting them into the foam.

Dried floral foam is a bit sandier in consistency than plastic foams. The best way to attach it is with hot glue. To cut the foam, simply use a serrated knife. To attach, first cut the foam to fit the shape of the container, allowing some space surrounding the foam, and glue into the basket, bag, or box.

Plastic foam. Styrofoam or plastic foam is a firm foam that can be used for either silk or dried materials. It is available in many different sizes and shapes, in green or white. The thinner stems of dried materials will need to be reinforced with a wood pick or floral-taped to a piece of stem wire to insert easily into this foam. Plastic foam can be attached with silicone or Crafter's Cement.

Wet floral foam. "Fresh" or wet floral foam (Oasis) is used for fresh flowers only. Do not attempt to use it for silk arrangements because it is very soft and will fall apart over a period of time after the arrangement is made. Any of the silk designs found in this book can also be done with fresh flowers, but you will need to replace the silk and dried foam with fresh foam. When decorating with fresh flowers and wet foam, be sure that you use a container that holds water.

To use fresh foam, place the foam block in water a few minutes until it sinks to the water level. Never force the block of foam under water; allow it to sink and absorb the water on its own. Cut the foam with a knife to the shape of the container. Wet foam can be attached with Oasis glue or with Oasis tape spread over the top of the foam and down the sides of the container.

MOSSES & FILLERS

Mosses and fillers are used to cover the foam so that it does not show. Never eliminate the moss/filler. You rarely notice them in a well-constructed arrangement, but you will surely notice a bare piece of foam through the flowers in a design. Mosses and fillers are also useful to embellish and decorate other areas of basket work, such as around the edge of the baskets or to fill space between items attached to the basket. Various types of fillers are available. Choose one that will best accent the design you are creating.

Spanish moss. For more natural-looking backgrounds, the gray color of Spanish moss is preferable. You can also find Spanish moss that has been dyed green but often this color is too bright and stands out against the other items rather than blending into the background.

Excelsior. This filler is a form of shredded wood shavings. Bleached excelsior is the most popular, although other colors are available. Excelsior is mostly used for country or kitchen designs, but it can be added to other designs for a unique color and texture change.

Natural moss. Found naturally on trees and rocks, this moss is peeled away, fumigated, and used for design work. It is available in natural, which has a brownish green look to it, or dyed. Like dyed Spanish moss, dyed natural moss tends to be too bright and, because it is more noticeable in the finished piece, it can detract from the overall design.

Shredded iridescent filler. Formed from iridescent plastic sheets, the most common manifestation of this filler is the grass used to fill Easter baskets. It is available in a number of different pastel colors and can be used in locations where it is an integral part of the design.

FLORAL TAPING

Floral tape is not a sticky tape. It is actually a waxed, crepe-paper material that sticks only to itself when stretched. Available in white, green, black, brown, and pastel colors, floral tape should coordinate with the colors used in the design. Choose pastel colors only when green or brown are inappropriate. Floral tape is useful when lengthening flower stems or attaching materials, such as clusters of dried flowers, to lengths of wire for insertion into designs.

To use: Hold the item or stems to be floral-taped in your left hand. Hold the roll of floral tape in your right hand, with the tape between your thumb and forefinger and the roll of tape resting on your little finger. Wrap the end of the floral tape around the top of the stem and squeeze so the end adheres to the tape and holds the stem.

Begin to twist the stem with your left hand, holding the tape firmly and stretching it slightly. The stretching helps to activate the adhesive abilities. Continue to turn the stem, stretching and angling the tape downward as you go (FIG. 1-1). Floral-tape all the way to the end of the stem, breaking and squeezing the tape at the end.

When lengthening or reinforcing stems, use 20-gauge wire at the necessary length, laying the wire next to the item to be taped so that the wire extends at least 1 inch (2.5 cm) beyond the end of the item. If the original flower stem is 3 inches (7.5 cm) or less, lay the wire next to the flower stem all the way up to the calyx (base) of the flower. Floral-tape the entire length of both stems together.

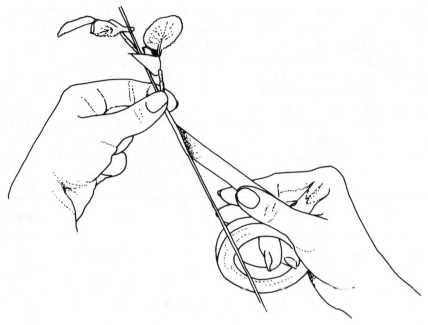

Fig. 1-1
Turn the flower stem as you
floral tape to the end of the
stem.

BASKETS

You can craft your own basket to fit the dimensions of your intended design, or you can select one of the many available in the market (FIG. 1-2). Several stores carry a selection of baskets to choose from; try craft shops, floral shops, and specialty gift shops as well as local discount stores and even flea markets. You might want to recycle a basket you've had around the house or even use an heirloom piece passed down from a beloved relative.

Select baskets with sturdy handles, since the recipient often will pick the basket up by the handle to transport it. Because the basket will weigh considerably more when filled, a handle that is not sturdy could break when lifted, spilling the contents to the ground.

Understand that the larger the basket, the more items you will need to fill it. Carefully plan the size of the basket based on what items you want to put inside. A basket that is too large will look empty if it is not filled properly, just as a basket that is too small will not adequately hold the gifts you want to include and will look out of balance and proportion.

If you want a basket in a color that is unavailable, you can try spraying one. Sprays can also add hints and dashes of color to highlight and spotlight the beauty of the basket. Design Master color tool sprays are my favorite for adding touches of color as well as for completely covering a basket.

Fig. 1-2
A wide variety of baskets
are available for decorating.

Other spray finishes available in the market include: stone finishes, whitewashing, cracked finishes, glazing, and webbing. All are available in spray cans for ease in applying to the baskets.

Stone finishes can give baskets the look of a variety of stones, including marble, quartz, alabaster, turquoise, and more. Whitewashing puts a transparent coat of white or other pale color on the basket (rubbing the whitewash spray while it is still wet helps some of the original color shine through the whitewashing). Cracked finishes (usually a two-part process) make the basket appear to have cracks throughout, much like peeling paint.

A variety of glazes are available—from high-gloss to matte to satin finishes. Webbing sprays are fun to use. They spray out a series of strings, which resemble spider webs, onto the finished item. The more spray you apply, the heavier the spider-web effect will appear. This type of product is available in a multitude of different colors, which can be used separately or mixed together.

BAGS

Decorated gift bags have hit the market by storm. With their ability to wrap a present quickly and easily, they have become a welcome alternative to traditional gift wrapping for millions of consumers.

A variety of photographic scenes—depicting everything from nature to cats to cars—are finding their way to prominence on the front of a gift

Fig. 1-3
Gift bags can be purchased plain or with graphic pictures and messages.

bag. Graphic designers are having a great deal of fun designing new bags for birthdays, anniversaries, Valentine's Day, and in several theme areas such as children, sports, "over the hill" and much more (FIG. 1-3).

Some of the newest gift lines on the market will also coordinate an entire gift ensemble with matching gift bags, gift boxes, mugs, cards, ribbons, and even balloons. When you decide on a theme for your gift bag, you'll find a lot to choose from.

Don't forget about plain bags. You'll find lunch-type bags available in all colors, many sizes and different widths. These provide a great deal of room for creative expression. You can add your own messages and embellish the bags to suit your needs.

Gift bags are simple to use, just insert gift items between layers of tissue paper before inserting into the gift bag. Allow the tissue paper to extend unevenly above the gift bag to add visual excitement. For a beautiful effect, use several colors of tissue paper that coordinate with the colors of the design, or tuck gifts down into the bag and surround them with shredding or other types of filler materials. Use one of the ideas contained in this book to finish off the bag, or put your imagination into high gear and design your own. It's fun and very, very easy.

BOXES

Like gift bags, gift boxes have become extremely popular and are, therefore, more readily available than ever before. You'll find a huge variety of designs and sizes available, many of which also coordinate with cards, balloons, and other gift items (FIG. 1-4).

In selecting a gift box, keep in mind the types of things you would like to put inside. If items will extend out of the box similar to what they would do in a basket or bag, you will need to choose a box with an open top. If the items you wish to give will be enclosed inside the box, the box will need to be large enough to accommodate these items.

Boxes can be filled with many of the same materials used for baskets and bags: tissue paper, shredding, and excelsior. Designs can be created on top of a closed box or inside an open box. Use floral foams and mosses to hold your design secure. Plain boxes are also available, and these allow for a great deal of creative expression. Feel free, too, to add hints or splashes of color to such bags.

BALLOONS

Balloons can often add a festive touch as well as a message to your chosen gift basket, bag, or box. Just the word *balloon* brings to mind cheerful, fun thoughts, and the bright colors and natural visual appeal of balloons make them a favorite of both children and adults (FIG. 1-5).

9

There are two types of balloons: latex and mylar. Latex balloons are made of a compound of synthetic rubber and are the least expensive of the two. They are available in a rainbow of colors in sizes ranging from 5 inches (12.5 cm) to 18 inches (45.5 cm).

Latex balloons can be filled with helium or with air. Air-filled balloons will not float, but they can be used as decorative accents to baskets, bags and boxes. Helium-filled balloons will float for about 8–12 hours, but they will float for several days if a liquid suspension agent was squirted inside the balloon before the helium was added. A suspension agent sticks to the walls of the balloon and traps helium from escaping from the porous walls of the balloon.

Mylar balloons are shiny, metallic-looking balloons, and they are available in a variety of sizes, shapes, designs, and colors. When properly sealed, a mylar balloon could float up to two weeks. In high-altitude areas, plain mylar balloons will show better floating results.

PLANNING YOUR GIFT BASKET, BAG, OR BOX

Follow this 10-step plan, and you'll be on your way to success in the area of creating spectacular gift containers.

1. *Selecting a theme.* Every basket should have a theme on which it is based. You may choose from general themes such as birthday, get well, new baby, or Christmas; or you may choose specific product themes such as fruit, wines, chocolates, etc. No matter what your theme, the gift container should be designed with a purpose in mind.

2. *Choosing colors.* Color is an exciting element of the overall look of the design, and it ties all the other elements into the chosen theme. Some color ideas include: red, white and blue for patriotic selections; red and white for pasta baskets; blue or pink for new babies; red and white for Valentine's day, etc. Remember if certain products do not conform to the colors you have chosen, you can wrap those items in colored papers or fabric so they match.

3. *Basket, bag, or box selection.* The selection of your container can either be made before the selection of the inside products or after. Either way, you will need to keep in mind how many things you want to put inside, the cost of those items, and the general theme. Therefore, if you choose the container first, select products that will fit inside; if you choose the contents first, be sure you select a container that will hold them all.

4. *Gift selection.* The items you select to fill your gift container may tie into the theme chosen through color or style. For example, you may include red-foil-wrapped chocolate hearts into a basket for their red color, or you may wish to include them because they tie into the theme "Chocolate Lover." Your whole basket may be based on the fact that you have one special gift you want to give in a unique way. The entire theme is then based on that featured item.

5. *Designing the shape.* Gift baskets should follow the rules of design and have a distinct form (shape), line, depth, and balance. The shape of your basket, box, or bag and its contents will assist in the selection of a shape for the design.

6. *Mechanics.* When designing a gift container all the mechanics (wires, glue, tape, etc.) should be invisible to the recipient. Care in forming the basket will permit you to hide all the unsightly necessities and to showcase the design and the gifts.

7. *Wrappings.* The wrapping should hold all the pieces of the basket together. If your design is well-created and secure, no overall wrapping is necessary. For security, you can wrap the entire piece in cellophane or netting, bunching the ends at the top of the basket. If wrappings are added, they should be included in the design and dec-

orated to coordinate. Unusual wrappings are also possible. We used a fishing net as a wrapping in one of the designs in this book (see color photograph, page 89).

8. *Finishing Touches.* Don't forget all the little extras that make a design complete. A few flowers, a tiny bow, the wonderful aroma of potpourri. Whatever fits and helps finish, add it.

9. *Cost.* It is important to consider cost as you begin to design the basket. Remember that both the inside contents of the design (gifts), as well as the container itself will all add up to the cost involved. Also, if the container for the gift can be reused, this supports a double-gift approach. If cost is of importance, keep careful count as you purchase items to complete the container as well as gifts to go inside. **Note:** The estimate given in the ''approximate cost'' section of each project relates only to those items used in the instructions. You will need to budget into your overall project the items you will use for the contents.

10. *Quality.* Always be sure to do the best possible work constructing and filling your basket, bag, or box. You want the recipient to feel the project was professionally executed.

Ribbons
& Bows

*T*his chapter will help you create all the wonderful ribbon embellishments found on the baskets, bags, and boxes throughout the book. Ribbons are available in a multitude of widths, colors, and textures. Use them wisely to compliment your gift design.

RIBBON LOOPS

To form a ribbon loop: Cut a piece of ribbon the length indicated in the directions. Bring the ends together and lay a wood pick next to the ends of the ribbon. Then wrap the wire snugly around the ribbon ends and the wood pick (FIG. 2-1).

Fig. 2-1
Bring the ends of a length of ribbon together to form a ribbon loop.

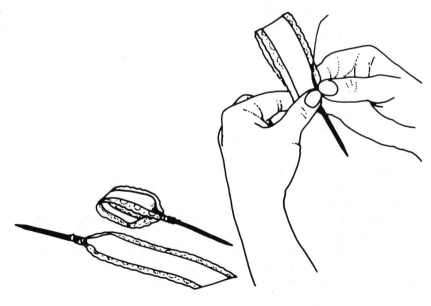

You can also use cloth-covered wire instead of a wood pick to secure the loop. After bringing the ribbon ends together, pinch them together to gather the ends. Then wrap a length of cloth-covered wire around the gathered ribbon ends, and twist the ends of the wire securely together.

RIBBON FANS

Ribbon fans are very easy to create and can be made many different sizes with different widths of ribbon. To form the fans, cut the ribbon the length specified in the instructions. Accordion-pleat each piece, using 1/2-inch (1.3 cm) pleats. After pleating, wrap a length of cloth-covered wire around one end to secure it, allowing the other end to fan out. The longer you cut the ribbon, the fuller the fan will be (FIG. 2-2).

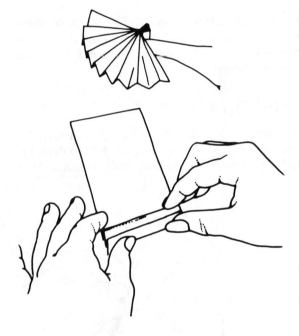

Fig. 2-2
Accordion-pleat wide ribbon to form a fan.

LACE TRIMS

Lace trims, available either gathered or ungathered, are often used to decorate gift baskets. Since I always gather them to surround the outside edge of a basket, I prefer to purchase them gathered. However, if you find a pattern you like or are unable to find gathered laces, it is easy enough to gather your own.

One way to achieve a gathered effect is simply to glue down little pleats of ribbon as you go around the edge of the basket. The easier way is to gather the ribbon in advance of gluing. You can do this with a gathering or basting stitch on the sewing machine, or by hand-basting a row of stitches across the top edge of the lace. Pull the threads to gather the lace. The more gathered you make the lace, the more lace you will need to surround the edge of the basket.

EMBELLISHED BOWS

By embellishing a bow, you can bring the elements of the design into the bow-making so that the two become more unified. After creating the bow following the instructions in this chapter, simply attach it to the basket, bag, or box you are working on. Then take small elements of the design—pieces and parts you are using elsewhere—and glue them into the center and throughout the loops of the bow. For example, if you are using small silk roses and pearl loops around the handle of the basket, take a few and glue them into the loops of the bow you have attached at the base of the handle. It creates a special look the recipient of your basket will love!

RIBBON BRAIDING

Fig. 2-3 (left)
Secure the ends of three lengths of ribbon before braiding.

Fig. 2-4 (right)
Bring the outside ribbon over the middle ribbon when braiding.

Braided ribbon adds a lovely accent to many finished designs. The procedure is the same as braiding hair. Begin by securing the ends of the three pieces of ribbon with cloth-covered wire as shown, or simply staple the three together (FIG. 2-3).

To braid: Bring the left ribbon over the center ribbon. The left ribbon is now the center ribbon. Bring the right ribbon over the center ribbon. The right ribbon is now the center ribbon. Repeat this process for the length of the ribbon you need, then secure the other ends of the ribbons with wire or staples (FIG. 2-4).

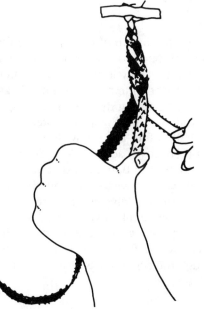

BASIC BOW

To form the type of bow pictured here (FIG. 2-5), begin by cutting a length of ribbon as indicated in the directions. Form a loop of ribbon the size necessary and hold it between the thumb and forefinger of your left hand (FIG. 2-6). If you are using a ribbon that has a right and wrong side, twist

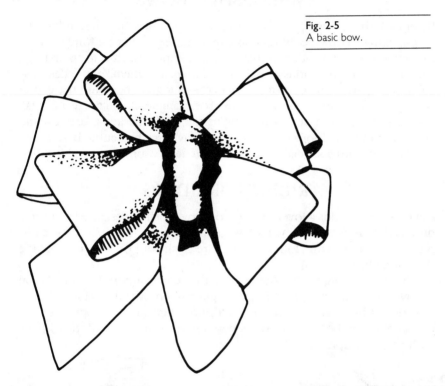

Fig. 2-5
A basic bow.

the bottom portion of the ribbon so that you see the right side (FIG. 2-7). Form a second loop with the lower portion of ribbon, bringing it to the back and pinching it between your thumb and forefinger (FIG. 2-8). Again twist the ribbon to see the right side and form a third loop. Continue in this fashion during the construction of one more loop.

After you have approximately one half the loops you are making, (two with a four-loop bow, four with a six-loop bow, and four with an eight-loop bow), add the loop in the center. To do this, simply form a small loop of ribbon around your thumb, and pinch the back portion of ribbon again between your thumb and forefinger (FIG. 2-9).

Continue adding the number of loops you will need to finish your bow (this should be two with a four-loop bow, two with a six-loop bow, and four with an eight-loop bow), in the same manner as described above. When finished, insert a cloth-covered wire or chenille stem through the center loop. Bring the ends to the back and twist securely.

Fig. 2-6 (right)
When beginning a bow, form one loop between your thumb and forefinger.

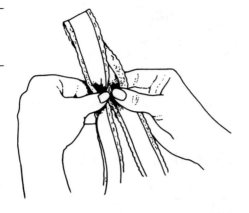

Fig. 2-7 (below)
If the ribbon is two-sided, twist it before forming the second loop.

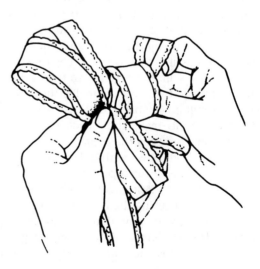

Fig. 2-8 (below, left)
Form a second loop and bring the ribbon back to the center.

Fig. 2-9 (below, right)
The center loop is formed by twisting the ribbon around your thumb.

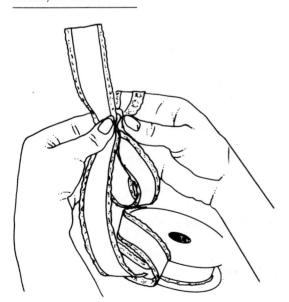

Bows Without Center Loops

At times the instructions will call for you to make a bow without a center loop. The reason for this is usually that you will be adding a small embellishment into the center of the bow, and having a loop in the center would conflict with the embellishment.

Simply follow the instructions above for a basic bow and eliminate the step for creating the center loop.

Using Ribbons Together in a Bow

Adding a variety of ribbons in each project makes the finished design exciting to look at and makes the project more unique. You can create bows with several ribbons in two ways.

The first way is simply to place all the ribbons you want to use one on top of the other and use them as though they were one ribbon. Follow the instructions for the bow you wish to create with the ribbons stacked on top of each other. After completing and securing the bow, pull the ribbons apart from each other and they will fluff out and fill a great deal of space.

The second way is easier to hold while creating. In this manner you will be forming each ribbon into a bow first, then attaching all the bows together. Follow the instructions for the Layered Bow below to learn all the details.

LAYERED BOW

A natural progression after the basic bow is a lovely bow style called the layered bow (FIG. 2-10). Throughout this book, you will find several projects in which two or more bows are used together in a design. This adds a great deal of contrast, texture, and color to the project.

After mastering the basic bow, the layered bow is simple! Make two basic bows as shown (FIG. 2-11). The one on the left will be the top bow. Its loops are slightly shorter than the back bow, and it has a center loop that was made from basic bow instructions. The bow on the right is the one that will be the back bow. Its loops are slightly larger, and it has no center loop. To make the "back bow," simply follow the basic bow instructions, omitting the center loop.

Secure both bows with either cloth-covered wire or a chenille stem. Insert the stems of the top bow through the loops of the bottom bow as shown (FIG. 2-12). Bring all the wires together behind, twisting them all together and securing the bows into one unit (FIG. 2-13).

You can create more than two layers simply by wiring as many bows as you wish, one on top of the other. Only the top bow should have a center loop; leave that step off of every other bow.

Fig. 2-10
A layered bow.

Fig. 2-11
To form a layered bow,
make separate bows first.

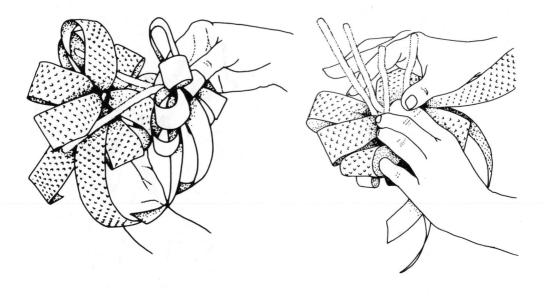

TAILORED BOW

The tailored bow has a long, narrow appearance when compared to the basic bow (FIG. 2-14). To form a tailored bow, you will be making a series of cylinders of ribbon. Each layer is a different length so that when stacked, they give a stair-step effect.

To form the cylinders, cut a length of ribbon, bringing the ends together and overlapping approximately 2 inches (5 cm), as shown (FIG. 2-15).

Form a series of smaller cylinders and stack on top of each other (FIG. 2-16). Lift this grouping and pinch together from both sides in the center of the bow (FIG. 2-17). Lay a length of ribbon the length desired on the back of the bow, and insert a chenille stem or cloth-covered wire through the center. Now bring both ends to the back of the bow, catching all loops and streamers, and twist the ends together tightly (FIG. 2-18).

Fig. 2-12 (above, left)
Bring the chenille stems of one bow through the loops of the other.

Fig. 2-13 (above, right)
Twist all the chenille stems together.

Fig. 2-14
A tailored bow.

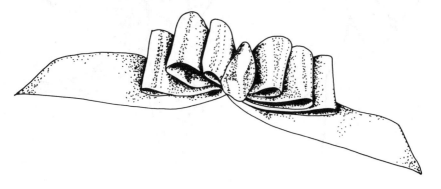

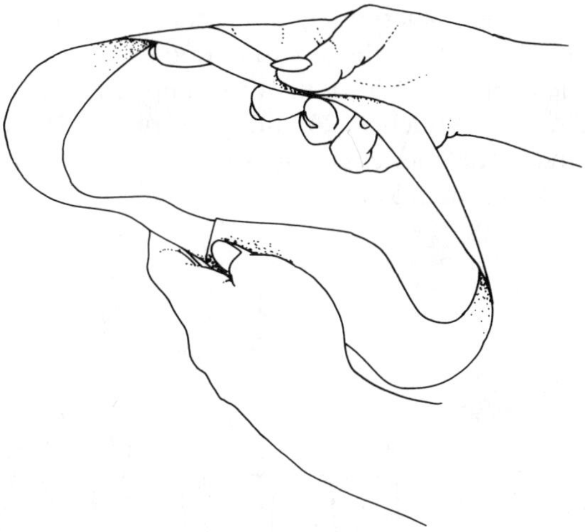

Fig. 2-15 (right)
Begin a tailored bow by
forming a cylinder.

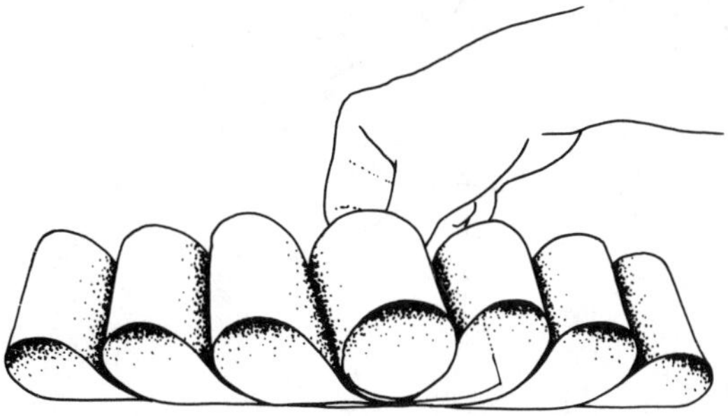

Fig. 2-16 (left)
Form several cylinders of
decreasing size.

Fig. 2-17 (right)
Pinch all the cylinders in the
center.

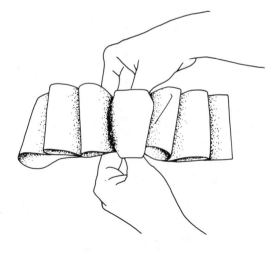

When determining how much ribbon to cut for each layer of loops, simply multiply the length of one loop by 4 and add 4 inches (10 cm) for the overlapped section. For example: For a 2-inch (5 cm) loop, multiply 2 × 4 = 8 inches (20 cm), + 4 inches (10 cm) = 12 inches (30.5 cm). Therefore, the length of your ribbon should be 12 inches (30.5 cm) to make a 2-inch loop.

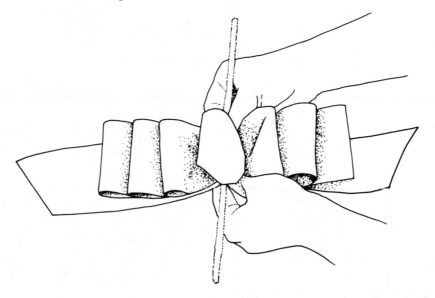

Fig. 2-18
Bring the chenille stem through the loops of the bow to secure.

Special Occasions

Many special moments in our lives call for special gifts. Personalizing a unique basket, bag, or box for birthdays, new babies, anniversaries, and bon voyage parties, to name only a few, will bring lots of joy and happiness into the lives of the recipients.

HAPPY BIRTHDAY BEAR BASKET

What a cute and simple way to quickly decorate a basket for a youngster's birthday! Adding small wrapped presents or candies complete the gift.

Beginner
15 minutes
$18 – $20

Without the little birthday flags, it would be a perfect gift basket for baby shower items and a charming decoration for baby's room. See color photograph on page 90.

You will need:

☐ One basket, 7 inches (17.5 cm) diameter × 3 inches (7.5 cm) deep × 12 inches (30.5 cm) tall

☐ Seven assorted-colored, flocked bears, 3 inches (7.5 cm) tall

☐ Five 1½-inch (4 cm) × 1-inch (2.5 cm) birthday and congratulations flags

☐ Glue

1. Glue two bears to the bottom side of the basket just below the basket handle. Apply glue to the bears at points where they will come in contact with the basket.

2. In the same manner, glue five bears to the side of the basket handle. Attach them in different body positions so they look like they are being playful. You might need to add to or subtract from the number of bears specified, depending on the size of your basket.

3. Glue the five birthday or congratulations flags in the paws of the five bears.

MYLAR PARTY BAG WITH PARTY FAVORS

This bag is a fun way to present a gift to a child or someone young at heart. A mylar party bag provides the wrappings, and party favors make up the decorations. See color photograph on page 90.

Beginner
10 minutes
$7 – $10

You will need:

☐ One mylar party bag, 7 inches (17.5 cm) × 18 inches (45.5 cm)

☐ One party hat

☐ One noisemaker

☐ One horn

☐ 2 yards (1.8 m) ¼-inch-wide (.6 cm) green metallic curling ribbon

☐ 2 yards (1.8 m) ¼-inch-wide (.6 cm) red metallic curling ribbon

☐ 2 yards (1.8 m) ¼-inch-wide (.6 cm) yellow curling ribbon

1. Cut ribbon in various lengths ranging from 12 inches (30.5 cm) to 24 inches (.6 m).

2. Tie lengths of ribbon around the gathered top of the bag.

3. Tie favors to the ends of the three longest ribbons.

4. Run the blade of a pair or scissors across the curling ribbon to curl.

HAPPY BIRTHDAY BASKET

Simple design techniques make this an easy basket to create. The same techniques could be used to design gift baskets for other special occasions. See color photograph on page 90.

Intermediate
30 minutes
$8 – $12

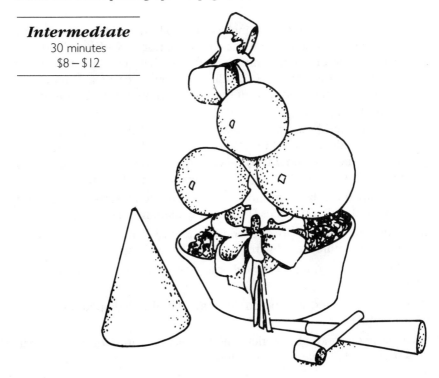

You will need:

- ☐ One round basket, 10 inches (25.5 cm) diameter, 4 inches (10 cm) deep × 15 inches (38 cm) tall
- ☐ Bright blue spray paint
- ☐ One 2-ounce bag foil confetti
- ☐ Spray glitter glue
- ☐ Three small latex balloons
- ☐ Three balloon sticks, 10 inches (25.5 cm) long
- ☐ 2¹⁄₂ yards (2.3 m) 1¹⁄₂-inch-wide (4 cm) multicolored polka dot ribbon
- ☐ 1¹⁄₂ yards (1.3 m) ⁷⁄₈-inch-wide (2 cm) screen-printed "Happy Birthday" ribbon
- ☐ Six assorted-color felt dinosaurs (If you can't find them already cut, follow the pattern given and cut them from felt.)
- ☐ Glue
- ☐ 30-gauge cloth-covered wire
- ☐ Three plastic balloon sticks, 10 inches long (25.5 cm)

1. Spray basket with bright blue paint. Allow to dry.
2. Spray outside of basket with glitter glue. Sprinkle on foil confetti. Allow to dry.
3. Cut 1 yard (.9 m) of the 1¹⁄₂-inch (4 cm) polka dot ribbon. Start at one side of the handle and attach one end of the ribbon with glue. Glue the ribbon at four different points on the basket handle. Allow the ribbon to loosely drape along the handle from one area of attachment to another. Glue the other end of the ribbon length on the opposite basket handle.
4. Make a layered bow using 1¹⁄₂ yards (1.3 m) of the polka dot ribbon and 1¹⁄₂ yards (1.3 m) of the "Happy Birthday" ribbon as directed on page 18. The bow should have six loops, each measuring 3 inches (7.5 cm) and having two 6-inch (15 cm) streamers. Set bow aside.
5. Blow up three latex balloons in three different sizes measuring 4 inches (10 cm) to 6 inches (15 cm). Tie balloons onto plastic sticks.
6. Secure the balloons to one side of the basket handle using a small length of cloth-covered wire. Trim away excess wire.
7. Glue the bow on top of the balloon sticks near the base of the basket handle.
8. Glue the felt dinosaurs randomly along the ribbon draped on the basket handle.
9. If desired, spray glitter glue on the balloons and sprinkle a small amount of foil confetti on the glue.

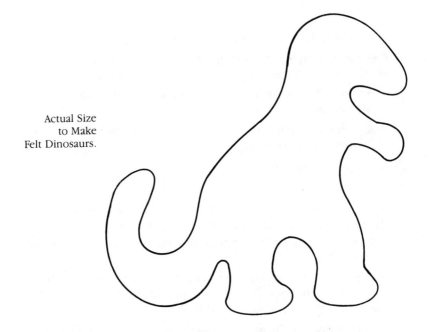

Actual Size
to Make
Felt Dinosaurs.

THANK YOU HOSTESS BASKET

Thank your hostess with a pretty basket decorated with ribbon, tulle, and flowers. Fill with your choice of gift items. It is a perfect expression of appreciation for any occasion. See color photograph on page 90.

Intermediate
45 minutes
$14 – $17

You will need:

- ☐ 2 yards (1.8 m) 6-inch-wide (15 cm) glittered peach tulle
- ☐ One peach oval basket, 9 inches (22.5 cm) × 8 inches (20 cm) diameter, 3 inches (7.5 cm) deep × 9 inches (22.5 cm) tall
- ☐ 2½ yards (2.3 m) ⅞-inch-wide (2 cm) screen-printed ivory "Thank You" ribbon
- ☐ Five stems miniature peach roses, each stem containing three 1-inch (2.5 cm) open roses and one bud
- ☐ 30-gauge cloth-covered wire
- ☐ Glue

1. At a point 3 inches (7.5 cm) from the end of the glittered tulle, gather the tulle together and secure it with a short length of cloth-covered wire. Glue the tulle at this gathering point to the middle of the top side of the basket.

2. In the same manner, gather and glue the tulle to the base of the basket handle. Loosely drape the tulle around the handle, and gather and glue the tulle at the top center of the basket handle.

3. Continue draping the tulle around the other side of the handle, gathering and gluing the tulle at the base of the opposite side of the basket handle.

4. Gather and glue the remaining tulle at a point on the side of the basket directly opposite the side you started. Trim excess tulle.

5. Cut a length of ribbon 1½ yards (1.3 m) long. Gather and glue in the same manner as the tulle. Trim excess ribbon.

6. Form a six-loop tailored bow with 1 yard (.9 m) of ribbon, following instructions on page 20. Secure the bow with cloth-covered wire. Glue the bow to the top center of the basket handle.

7. Glue two stems of the miniature peach roses to each side of the basket handle. Position one stem going up the handle, and glue it in place. Position the other stem along the edge of the basket, and glue it in place.

8. Cut the flowers and leaves off the last stem of flowers. Glue the roses and leaves to the middle of the top of each side of the basket at the point where the tulle and ribbon are gathered and glued.

BON VOYAGE BASKET

Not only would this basket be a fun way to say "Bon Voyage" to friends heading off on a Carribbean vacation, but it would also make an effective centerpiece for a summer tropical party. A tropical-print bow colorfully compliments a basket gathered with fishnet to which seashells are attached. For a gift basket, add suntan lotion, sunglasses, and all the other necessary accessories to complete the fun. See color photograph on page 89.

Advanced
2 hours
$20 – $25

You will need:

- ☐ One whitewashed basket, 10 inches (25.5 cm) diameter × 18 inches (45.5 cm) tall × 8 inches (20 cm) deep
- ☐ 2^1/$_2$ yards (2.3 m) 2^1/$_2$-inch (6.5 cm) wide tropical-print ribbon
- ☐ 5-foot-square piece fishnet
- ☐ Twenty-four assorted seashells
- ☐ One 6-inch (15 cm) starfish
- ☐ One stem white orchids with four flowers 3 inches (7.5 cm) wide
- ☐ Two plastic Hawaiian leis, one red and one blue
- ☐ Three 3^1/$_2$-inch-long (8.8 cm) dried pods
- ☐ Three ^{1}/$_4$-inch (.6 cm) pearls
- ☐ Twelve silk spider-plant leaves, each 5 inches (12.5 cm) long
- ☐ Glue
- ☐ 30-gauge cloth-covered wire

1. Lay fishnet flat on the table. Place basket on top of the net, directly in the center.

2. Secure the net in place with cloth-covered wire at the top left of the basket handle. Allow the rest of the net to drape freely.

3. Make a six-loop basic bow using 2 yards (1.8 m) of the tropical-print ribbon, following instructions on page 16. Each loop should measure 4 inches (10 cm) long with two streamers that measure 6 inches (15 cm) each.

4. Secure the bow with cloth-covered wire to the left side of the base of the basket handle.

5. Attach the three pods to the basket by gluing them to the handle and rim of the basket.

6. Glue the spray of orchids to the basket handle. Place the stem of orchids behind the bow. The orchids will curve up the basket handle.

7. Randomly glue 10 spider-plant leaves around the bow and in between the orchids. Trim the stems of the leaves if necessary.

8. Randomly glue 12 seashells to the fishnet around the rim and handle of the basket.

9. Fill the basket with gift items.

10. Glue the large starfish and two spider plant leaves to the base of the basket handle on the opposite side of the basket.

11. Gather the fishnet together and secure it with cloth-covered wire to the top right side of the basket handle.

12. Use lengths of cloth-covered wire to secure the plastic leis to the basket handle at the net's gathering spot.

13. Glue the remaining 12 seashells around the basket and onto the netting.

14. Make a 2-inch (5 cm) loop and two streamers, one streamer measuring 3 inches (7.5 cm) and one measuring 6 inches (15 cm), with 1/2 yard (.5 m) of tropical print ribbon. Secure this with cloth-covered wire. Glue to the outside of the basket just below the starfish.

STARS AND STRIPES

This cleverly decorated basket would make a wonderful welcome-home statement for a member of the armed services who is returning from military duty. Or you could fill it with goodies for a Fourth of July celebration. See color photograph on page 89.

You will need:

☐ One rectangular basket, 10 inches (25.5 cm) × 6 inches (15 cm) diameter, 5 inches (12.5 cm) deep

Intermediate
45 minutes
$17 – $20

- [ ] 2¹/₂ yards (2.3 m) ⁵/₈-inch-wide (1.5 cm) red wire-edged ribbon
- [ ] 1 yard (.9 m) royal blue mum bow ribbon (ribbon already fringed with draw string to form bow)
- [ ] 1 yard (.9 m) iridescent mini mum bow ribbon
- [ ] One 5-inch (12.5 cm) square of red metallic cardboard (or 5-inch red metallic star)
- [ ] One 5-inch (12.5 cm) square of silver metallic cardboard (or 5-inch silver metallic star)
- [ ] One 5-inch (12.5 cm) square of blue metallic cardboard (or 5-inch blue metallic star)
- [ ] Three 1-inch (2.5 cm) paper American flags
- [ ] Two white chenille stems
- [ ] One package red, white, and blue wired star garland
- [ ] Glue
- [ ] 30-gauge cloth-covered wire

1. Glue basket lid into an open position.
2. Make an eight-loop bow with 2 yards (1.8 m) of the wired star garland, following instructions on page 16. Each loop should measure 3 inches (7.5 cm). Secure the bow with cloth-covered wire.
3. Make a four-loop bow using 1 yard (.9 m) of the wired star garland.
4. Glue the four-loop bow to the right top corner of the outside of the basket.

5. Glue the eight-loop bow to the left top back corner of the basket.

6. Make two bows, using 1¹/₄ yards (1.1 m) red wired ribbon for each bow. Each bow should have eight loops 2 inches (5 cm) long and two 6-inch (15 cm) streamers. Secure with cloth-covered wire. Glue one bow to the center of each star garland bow already attached to the basket.

7. Cut two 18-inch (45.5 cm) lengths of royal blue mum bow ribbon. Grab the strings on each end of the length of ribbon and pull together to form the mum. Tie the ends to keep its shape. Glue one bow to the center of each red wired ribbon bow.

8. Cut two 18-inch (45.5 cm) lengths of iridescent mini mum ribbon. Make two bows as directed above. Glue one to the center of each royal blue mum bow.

9. Glue one 3-inch (7.5 cm) length of chenille stem to each cardboard star. Glue the chenille stem of two of the stars to the inside of the left corner cluster of bows. Glue the third star in the same manner to the right front corner cluster of bows.

10. Glue two small American flags to the left back corner cluster of bows and one small flag to the right front corner cluster of bows. If you choose, wrap the remaining star garland around the basket.

OVER THE HILL BASKET

Intermediate
45 minutes
$15 – $18

You can create a pretty basket to tease an aging friend. But be prepared—your time will come, so be kind! See color photograph on page 88.

You will need:

☐ One basket, 8 inches (20 cm) diameter, 9 inches (22.5 cm) tall × 3 inches (7.5 cm) deep

☐ Silver spray paint

☐ Black spray paint

☐ 2 yards (1.8 m) 1¼-inch-wide (3.1 cm) white/black/silver plaid ribbon

☐ 3 yards (2.7 m) ⅞-inch-wide (2 cm) black "Over the Hill" ribbon

☐ One stem silk carnations with six 1½-inch (4 cm) flowers

☐ Twelve English Ivy leaves, 1½ (4 cm) wide

☐ Eighteen stems glittered black ting ting (a long, thin dried material)

☐ 2 yards (1.8 m) 6-inch-wide (15 cm) black tulle

☐ Black "Over the Hill" mylar balloon

☐ Cloth-covered wire

☐ Glue

1. Cut a 1¼-yard (1.1 m) length of the plaid ribbon. Make a six-loop tailored bow as directed on page 16. The loops should be in graduated lengths of 2 inches (5 cm), 2½ inches (6.5 cm), and 3 inches (7.5 cm). Streamers should be 3 inches (7.5 cm) long. Glue this bow with the loops positioned vertically at the base of one side of the basket handle.

2. Make two 3-inch (7.5 cm) ribbon loops using 6 inches (15 cm) of the plaid ribbon for each, as directed on page 20.

3. Using 12 inches (30.5 cm) of the same ribbon, make a single 3-inch-long (7.5 cm) ribbon loop with a 6-inch (15 cm) streamer.

4. Glue the two ribbon loops without the streamer on the basket handle in an upward direction, 2 inches (5 cm) apart. Glue the last loop with the streamer attached 2 inches (5 cm) away from the last single loop. The streamer should curve over the other side of the basket handle.

5. Cut two ½-yard (.5 m) lengths of the "Over the Hill" ribbon. Make two four-loop bows with no center loop as directed on page 18. Each loop should measure 2 inches (5 cm) long. Glue one bow to each side of the tailored plaid bow near the base of the basket handle.

6. Cut six 12-inch (30.5 cm) lengths of "Over the Hill" ribbon. Use each length to make a single ribbon loop. Glue the loops randomly to the basket handle filling the spaces between the plaid ribbon loops.

7. Spray carnation heads black. Allow to dry.

8. Remove the carnation heads from the main stem of the flower. Glue

them randomly between the ribbon loops attached to the basket handle.

9. Cut the English Ivy leaves apart from the main stem of the foliage. Glue them randomly between the ribbon loops and the carnations attached to the basket handle.

10. Cut the ting ting into lengths varying from 3 inches (7.5 cm) to 10 inches (25.5 cm). Glue these randomly throughout the design created by the ribbon loops, carnations, and ivy.

11. Using the black tulle, make an eight-loop bow without a center loop. Each loop should measure 4 inches (10 cm) long. Secure with cloth-covered wire. Glue to the inside of the basket near the base of the handle directly behind the ribbon and flowers.

IT'S A BOY GIFT BAG

A bow embellished with a fuzzy brown bear adds a sweet finished look to this decorated bag. A rattle or baby toy could be added in place of the bear. See color photograph on page 88.

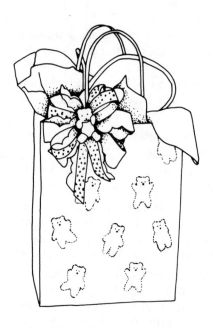

Beginner
15 minutes
$7 – $10

You will need:

☐ 1 yard (.9 m) 1¼-inch-wide (3.1 cm) "It's a Boy" ribbon

☐ 1 yard (.9 m) ⅝-inch-wide (1.5 cm) blue polka dot ribbon

☐ One gift bag with bears, 8½ inches (21.3 cm) × 11 inches (28 cm)

☐ One 2-inch (5 cm) flocked brown bear

☐ Glue

☐ 30-gauge cloth-covered wire

1. Following the instructions on page 18, form a layered bow with both of the listed ribbons. Each ribbon should have six 2½-inch-long (6.5 cm) loops and six 4-inch (10 cm) streamers.

2. Attach the cloth-covered wire from the bow to the base of the bag's handle.

3. Glue the bear to the center of the bow.

IT'S A GIRL GIFT BASKET

This basket will make a very pretty accent piece in a little girl's room after the gift items are used. It could also be easily adapted for a romantic look by simply substituting the ''It's a Girl'' ribbon for a plain satin or lace ribbon. See color photograph on page 93.

Intermediate
30 minutes
$12 – $15

You will need:

☐ One oval basket, 8 inches (20 cm) × 6 inches (15 cm) diameter × 10 inches (25.5 cm) tall × 3½ inches (8.8 cm) deep

☐ 1 yard (.9 m) 5-inch-wide (12.5 cm) gathered ivory/mauve lace

☐ 2 yards (1.8 m) $5/8$-inch-wide (1.5 cm) pink polka dot ribbon

☐ 2 yards (1.8 m) $1/16$-inch-wide (.1 cm) mauve satin tubing

☐ 2 yards (1.8 m) $1/16$-inch-wide (.1 cm) ivory satin tubing

☐ Eight 1-inch (2.5 cm) premade ivory bows with pearl in center

☐ 1 yard (.9 m) $11/4$-inch-wide (3.1 cm) "It's a Girl" screen-printed ribbon

☐ Glue

☐ 30-gauge cloth-covered wire

1. Glue the gathered lace around the top edge of the basket. Allow $11/2$ inches (4 cm) of the lace to extend above the edge of the basket.

2. Cut a 1-yard (.9 m) length of mauve satin tubing, ivory satin tubing, and pink polka dot ribbon. Make a layered bow using these three lengths of ribbon as directed on page 18. Each ribbon should have six loops $21/2$ inches (6.5 cm) long and two 3-inch (7.5 cm) streamers. Do not add a center loop to this bow.

3. Repeat forming a second bow as described in step 2. Set these two aside.

4. With the "It's a Girl" ribbon, form a six-loop bow as directed on page 16. Each loop should be $21/2$ inches (6.5 cm) long with two 3-inch (7.5 cm) streamers. Set bow aside.

5. Use approximately 1 yard (.9 m) of the polka dot ribbon to cover the basket handle. Start by gluing one end of the ribbon to one side of the basket handle. Wrap the ribbon around the handle to completely cover it, and glue the other end to the opposite side of the basket handle. Trim away excess ribbon.

6. Using 1 yard (.9 m) each of the mauve and ivory satin tubing, glue to one side of the basket handle. Loosely twist the two lengths together, and wrap it around the basket handle. Glue the ends to the other side of the handle. Trim excess tubing.

7. Glue one layered bow at each side of the base of the basket handle.

8. Glue the "It's a Girl" bow to the top center of the basket handle.

9. Glue the eight premade satin bows with pearls, evenly spaced, to the basket handle.

ANNIVERSARY BASKET

This basket would be a lovely remembrance of a special anniversary. Fill the basket with happy memories, old photos, letters, and more to make it personalized. See color photograph on page 88.

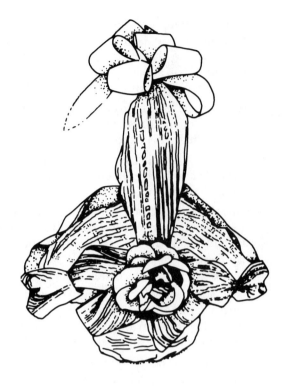

Intermediate
45 minutes
$13 – $17

You will need:

☐ One white, willow, princess-style basket; 7 inches (17.5 cm) × 9 inches (22.5 cm) diameter × 10 inches (25.5 cm) tall × 4 inches (10 cm) deep

☐ 2 yards (1.8 m) $2^3/_4$-inch-wide (6.8 cm) silver/gold striped lamé ribbon

☐ $1^1/_2$ yards (1.3 m) $1^3/_8$-inch-wide (3.4 cm) "Happy Anniversary" silk-screened ribbon

☐ Two gold lamé open roses with gold leaves, roses measuring $2^1/_2$ inches (6.5 cm) diameter

☐ Glue

☐ Cloth-covered wire

1. Cut lamé ribbon into two 27-inch (.3 m) lengths. (This might vary slightly according to the size of the basket.)

2. Using one of the lengths of lamé ribbon, gather it together with cloth-covered wire at a point 3 inches (7.5 cm) from the end of the ribbon. Glue this gathered spot to the base of the side of the basket handle. Allow the 3-inch (7.5 cm) section to drape down the side of the basket.

3. At three different points on one half of the top side of the basket rim, put a dab of glue. Gently and carefully pinch the lamé ribbon together and attach to the basket rim at the point where the glue has been applied. If you are using hot glue, apply the glue to one point at a time since it cools quickly.

4. Repeat steps 2 and 3 to cover the other half of the basket rim. Allow the ends of the ribbon to overlap where they come together at the base of the basket handle.

5. Using the remaining 18 inches (45.5 cm) of the lamé ribbon, gather 2 inches (5 cm) from each end with cloth-covered wire in the same manner as described in step 2.

6. Glue the gathered point of this ribbon length at the base of one side of the basket handle. Apply a dab of glue to the center of the basket handle and pinch the lamé ribbon together, attaching the ribbon to the handle in this manner. Glue the other end of the ribbon to the opposite side of the basket handle.

7. Make an eight-loop bow using 1 1/2 yards (1.3 m) of the "Happy Anniversary" ribbon as directed on page 16. Each loop should measure 2 1/2 inches (6.5 cm) long with two 3-inch (7.5 cm) streamers. Glue this bow to the center top of the basket handle.

8. Glue one gold lamé rose with leaves to each side of the basket handle. This should cover all exposed wires.

DUFFER'S GIFT BAG

This bag was cleverly decorated with special-interest gift items inside and out, all aimed at the person who lives and loves golf. You could easily adapt this idea to any gift-bag theme. See color photograph on page 88.

You will need:

☐ One golf-theme gift bag, 8 inches (20 cm) × 10 inches (25.5 cm)
☐ Three practice golf balls
☐ Three golf tees
☐ 2 yards (1.8 m) 5/8-inch-wide (1.5 cm) green satin ribbon
☐ 2 1/2 yards (2.3 m) 1/8-inch-wide (.3 cm) blue satin ribbon
☐ 2 1/2 yards (2.3 m) 1/8-inch-wide (.3 cm) yellow satin ribbon
☐ 30-gauge cloth-covered wire
☐ Glue

1. Make a layered bow as directed on page 16, using 2 yards (1.8 m) each of the green, blue, and yellow satin ribbon. Each ribbon will have 12 loops measuring 2 inches (5 cm) to 2 1/2 inches (6.5 cm) long and

Beginner
20 minutes
$10–$12

4-inch-long (10 cm) to 6-inch-long (15 cm) streamers. Secure with cloth-covered wire.

2. Cut ¹/₂ yard (.5 m) of the blue ribbon and ¹/₂ yard (.5 m) of the yellow ribbon into several different lengths measuring from 6 inches (15 cm) to 9 inches (22.5 cm).

3. Tie the tees and practice balls to the ends of these separate lengths.

4. Use the cloth-covered wire to secure the bow to the handle of the gift bag.

5. Glue the ends of the lengths of ribbon with balls and tees attached to the center of the bow. Allow the tees and practice balls to drape down the front of the bag.

Romantic Designs

Soft, delicate, and lacy are the words that best describe the designs in this chapter. With many styles to choose from, you'll find just what you need for a wedding, shower or even just a quiet evening at home with the one you love.

LACE AND RIBBON ROSE BASKET

If necessary, you could easily change the colors used for this basket to coordinate its appearance to suit different occasions or have additional uses after the gift items are removed. See color photograph on page 87.

Beginner
1 hour
$24 – $28

You will need:

- [ ] One natural-color basket, 12 inches (30.5 cm) × 15 inches (38 cm) diameter × 18 inches (45.5 cm) tall × 7 inches (17.5 cm) deep
- [ ] 1 1/2 yards (1.3 m) 1 1/2-inch-wide (4 cm) pink/white gathered lace
- [ ] 3 1/2 yards (3.2 m) 2 1/2-inch-wide (6.5 cm) blue gathered lace
- [ ] 5 1/2 yards (5 m) 1/8-inch-wide (.3 cm) pink satin ribbon with silver edge
- [ ] 5 1/2 yards (5 m) 1/2-inch-wide (1.3 cm) sheer blue iridescent ribbon
- [ ] Sixteen 3/4-inch-wide (1.8 cm) pink satin ribbon roses with leaves
- [ ] Fourteen 1/2-inch-wide (1.3 cm) blue satin ribbon roses with leaves
- [ ] Glue
- [ ] 30-gauge cloth-covered wire

1. Measure the circumference of the basket (the area around the outside edge of the basket). Ours measured 30 inches (.8 m). Cut a length of the blue gathered lace the same measurement. Glue this length of lace around the top edge of the basket rim. The lace should drape slightly over the outside edge of the basket.

2. Glue a length of the pink/white lace in the same manner as described in step 1. This lace should be placed directly on top of the blue lace.

3. Measure the length of the basket handle from one end across the top to the other end. Ours measured 28 inches (.7 m). Cut two pieces of the blue gathered lace to the length determined by the measurement of the basket handle. Glue the straight edge of the blue lace to the top center area of the basket handle. Repeat with the second length of blue lace, gluing it in the same manner on the other side of the handle. Allow the straight edges of each lace piece to slightly overlap in the center of the handle.

4. Cut 2 yards (1.8 m) each of the blue sheer ribbon and pink/silver ribbon. Glue one end of each of these ribbons near the base of one side of the basket handle.

5. At intervals of approximately 3 inches (7.5 cm), gently loop and then glue the two ribbons to the top edge of the gathered lace. Continue around the entire top of the basket rim.

6. Cut 1 1/2 yards (1.3 m) each of the blue sheer ribbon and the pink/silver ribbon. Glue one end of each of these ribbons near the base of one side of the basket handle.

7. At intervals of approximately 4 inches (10 cm), loop and glue the ribbons in the same manner as described in step 5 along the top of the basket handle.

8. Cut 2 yards (1.8 m) each of the blue sheer ribbon and the pink/silver ribbon. Make a layered bow as directed on page 18. Each bow should

have 10 loops, each 2 inches (5 cm) long with two 15-inch (38 cm) streamers. Glue the bow to the top center of the basket handle.

9. Glue the ribbon roses at the points where the ribbons are attached to the basket. Alternate the color of the roses when gluing to the basket.

ROMANTIC VICTORIAN BASKET

This would make a stunning shower gift for a bride-to-be. It could be designed with her bedroom colors. Fill it with romantic gifts, such as lotions, perfumed bath crystals, sachets, and more! See color photograph on page 87.

> **_Advanced_**
> 3 hours
> $60 – $70

You will need:

☐ One large ivory basket, 20 inches (50.5 cm) diameter × 22 inches (55.5 cm) tall × 9 inches (22.5 cm) deep

☐ 2 yards (1.8 m) 4-inch-wide (10 cm) ivory gathered lace

- ☐ 4 yards (3.6 m) 4-inch-wide (10 cm) ivory lace ribbon (for shirring on handle)
- ☐ 10 yards (9 m) 4-inch-wide (10 cm) ivory lace ribbon (for gathering down the center)
- ☐ 2 yards (1.8 m) 1¹/2-inch-wide (4 cm) peach moiré ribbon
- ☐ 4 yards (3.6 m) ⁵/8-inch-wide (1.5 cm) sheer, sparkling, peach ribbon
- ☐ 4 yards (3.6 m) 2 mm fused pearls
- ☐ 4 yards (3.6 m) ¹/8-inch-wide (.3 cm) peach satin tubing
- ☐ ¹/2 yard (.5 m) 5-inch-wide (12.5 cm) peach lace
- ☐ ¹/3 yard (.3 m) 5-inch-wide (12.5 cm) aqua lace
- ☐ 2¹/2 yards (2.3 m) 6-inch-wide (15 cm) peach tulle
- ☐ ¹/2 yard (.5 m) 6-inch-wide (15 cm) aqua tulle
- ☐ One 10-inch (25.5 cm) ivory crochet hat
- ☐ Six 2-inch (5 cm) pearl loops
- ☐ Four 1-inch (2.5 cm) ivory ribbon roses
- ☐ Six 1-inch (2.5 cm) peach ribbon roses
- ☐ Small bunch aqua preserved, dried baby's breath
- ☐ 1¹/2 yards (1.3 m) 2 mm peach fused pearls
- ☐ 1¹/2 yards (1.3 m) 2 mm ivory fused pearls
- ☐ 1¹/2 yards (1.3 m) 2 mm white fused pearls
- ☐ ¹/2 yard (.5 m) 1¹/2 inch-wide (4 cm) peach lace-edged ribbon
- ☐ 1 yard (.9 m) ¹/8-inch-wide (.3 cm) aqua picette ribbon
- ☐ 2 ounces rose potpourri (or another fragrance of your choice)
- ☐ Glue
- ☐ 32-gauge white cloth-covered wire

1. Glue the 4-inch-wide (10 cm) gathered lace around the outside edge of the rim of the basket.
2. Glue one end of the 1¹/2-inch-wide (4 cm) peach moiré ribbon to one side of the basket handle. Wrap the ribbon around the handle to cover it completely. Glue the other end of the ribbon at the other side of the handle.
3. Take 4 yards (3.6 m) of the 4-inch-wide (10 cm) lace ribbon and glue one end around one end of the handle. You will glue the ribbon together to form a cylinder completely enclosing the handle. Continue to glue the ribbon around the handle so that the cylinder you are preparing is covering the handle. Push the ribbon down as you go, and it will gather along the handle. When all the ribbon has been glued on, rearrange the gathers so they uniformly cover the handle of the basket.

4. Gather 10 yards (9 m) of 4-inch-wide (10 cm) ribbon down the center of the lace. Pull the threads of the ribbon to gather it tightly. The finished gathered lace should fit around the top edge of the basket. Be sure to measure your basket to be exact. Our basket had a 60-inch circumference.
5. Braid the 4 yards (3.6 m) of 5/8-inch (1.5 cm) sheer sparkling ribbon, the 2 mm fused pearls, and the satin tubing as directed on page 15. Glue the braid to the center of the gathered lace in step 4. Secure the ends, and trim away any excess braid.

Hat Embellishment

1. Glue the peach-and-lace ribbon around the crown of the crochet hat. Make a six-loop bow with 1 yard (.9 m) of peach tulle as directed on page 16. The loops should measure 2 inches (5 cm). Glue the bow to cover the joining point of peach-and-lace ribbon. Attach small pieces of the baby's breath on each side of the bow on the hat. Extend the baby's breath to cover about a 4-inch-wide (10 cm) area of the hat.
2. Cut the stems of the ribbon roses 1 inch (2.5 cm) long. Glue three peach roses and two ivory roses to each side of the bow, evenly between the baby's breath. Glue two pearl loops within the design formed by the baby's breath and ribbon roses.
3. Make two 6-inch (15 cm) lace fans and three 6-inch (15 cm) peach lace fans as directed on page 14.
4. Glue fans to the basket handle and rim of basket, then glue the hat to the center of the fans.
5. Glue the ends of the three 1 1/2-yard (1.3 m) pearl lengths (peach, ivory, white) about 9 inches (22.5 cm) up the handle from the basket edge.
6. Drape the pearls over the handle (leave some hanging down), over the fans and the hat. Secure at the rim of the basket just at the edge of the hat. Leave about 9 inches (22.5 cm) of two pearl strands over the edge of the basket.

Potpourri Sacks

1. Cut two 6-inch-wide (15 cm) × 9-inch-wide (22.5 cm) pieces of aqua tulle and two 6-inch (15 cm) × 9-inch (22.5 cm) pieces of peach tulle. Place a mound of potpourri inside each. Tie each sack with 9 inches (22.5 cm) of aqua ribbon.
2. Glue one potpourri sack to cover the glued ends of the draped pearls on the handle.
3. Tie potpourri sacks to draped pearls hanging over the edge of the basket.

4. Use the leftover braided ribbon to create a small bow as directed on page 18. Glue this bow under the potpourri sacks at the rim of the basket.

5. Glue one pearl loop by each potpourri sack.

WEDDING CARD BASKET

Lace and pearls combine to create a very elegant and romantic look for this basket. It would be an eye-catching table decoration for any wedding reception and would serve a useful purpose, too, as a container for loose wedding card-gifts. You may customize this design by using colors of your choice. See color photograph on page 87.

Advanced
3 hours
$80 – $90

You will need:

☐ One oval basket, 16 inches (40.5 cm) × 18 inches (45.5 cm) diameter × 20 inches (50.5 cm) tall × 7 inches (17.5 cm) deep

☐ 2 yards (1.8 m) 5-inch-wide (12.5 cm) gathered lace

☐ 5¹/₂ yards (5 m) 3-inch-wide (7.5 cm) white iridescent brocade ribbon

☐ 4 yards (3.6 m) 4-inch-wide (10 cm) white lace ribbon

☐ 4 yards (3.6 m) 1³/₈-inch-wide (3.4 cm) white iridescent striped ribbon

☐ 4 yards (3.6 m) 6-inch-wide (15 cm) white glitter-sparkled tulle

☐ Six 2¹/₂-inch-wide (6.5 cm) white iridescent cloth flowers with pearls

☐ Two 10-inch-long (25.5 cm) white cloth flower spray with pearls

☐ Eight 12-inch-long (30.5 cm) white cloth mini flower and pearl spray

☐ Two 4¹/₂-inch-wide (11.3 cm) white cloth iridescent orchids

☐ Thirty-six 1¹/₂-inch-long (4 cm) green silk leaves

☐ Twelve 1-inch-long (2.5 cm) green silk leaves

☐ Six 18-inch-long (45.5 cm) iridescent lily-of-the-valley hanging flower sprays (each spray containing six stems of drooping flowers)

☐ Six 4-inch-long (10 cm) white cloth lily-of-the-valley hanging flower sprays (each spray containing two stems of drooping flowers)

☐ Twelve 1¹/₂-inch (4 cm) mauve and pearl flowers (or other color of your choice)

☐ Glue

☐ 30-gauge cloth-covered wire

1. With glue, attach the 2-yard (1.8 m) length of 5-inch (12.5 cm) lace around the outside of the basket, just under the lip of the basket.

2. Cut a 1¹/₂-yard (1.3 m) length of the 3-inch (7.5 cm) white iridescent brocade ribbon, and glue it at one side of the basket handle. Wrap around the handle to completely cover. Glue the other end at the opposite end of the handle and trim excess ribbon.

3. With 4 yards (3.6 m) each of 4-inch (10 cm) white lace ribbon and 1³/₈-inch (3.4 cm) white iridescent striped ribbon and 6 inches (15 cm) white sparkled tulle, make a very loose braid as on page 15.

4. Glue this braid to the top edge of the basket and over the top of the handle. Glue the braid loosely; do not flatten it.

5. With 2 yards (1.8 m) of the 3-inch (7.5 cm) white brocade ribbon, make a tailored bow as directed on page 20. The three sets of loops should measure 4 inches (10 cm), 3¹/₂ inches (8.8 cm), and 3 inches (7.5 cm) with 8-inch (20 cm) streamers. Repeat to make another bow with the same dimensions.

6. Glue the two bows made in step 5 to the base of each side of the basket handle.

7. Glue the two orchids to the top center of the basket handle. Overlap them slightly.

8. Glue the two 10-inch (25.5 cm) cloth flower sprays with pearls, one on each side of the two orchids on top of the handle. Position the stem of the spray underneath the orchids.

9. Glue three of the 18-inch (45.5 cm) lily-of-the-valley sprays. Position the stems under the 10-inch (25.5 cm) flower sprays. Allow the lily of the valley to drape along the basket handle and cascade over the bow. Repeat this step on the other side of the handle.

10. Position the eight 12 inch-wide (30.5 cm) mini flower and pearl

sprays around the outside edge of the basket next to the lace-and-ribbon braid. Equally space the flower sprays, and attach with glue.

11. Equally space the 2½-inch (6.5 cm) single iridescent flowers around the basket edge in between the flower sprays. Glue to hold this in place.

12. Glue the 4-inch (10 cm) lily-of-the-valley sprays directly underneath the flowers attached to the basket in step 11.

13. Glue the mauve flowers and the two sizes of leaves randomly throughout the design of the basket.

BRIDAL SHOWER GROUPING

The color scheme of ivory and gold combined with the textures of lace and pearls create a stunningly elegant and romantic look for these gift bags and accessory pieces. Used as a grouping, these gift bags would make a lovely centerpiece to be used for a bridal shower. Not only will there be the gifts of a floral arrangement and corsage for the bride, but the smaller bags will contain hairpieces for the bridesmaids and flower girls. See color photograph on page 87.

Bridal Bag with Corsage

Advanced
6 hours (whole grouping)
Bridal Bag w/corsage:
$19 – $22
Floral design:
$43 – $48
Bridal Bag w/haircomb:
$20 – $24
Bridal Bag w/hairclip:
$13 – $15

You will need:

- ☐ Three ivory satin roses with 1¹/2-inch-wide (4 cm) heads
- ☐ Twelve ivory circular pearl loops, 2 inches (5 cm)
- ☐ Six gold pearl sprays, 2¹/2 inches (6.5 cm) long
- ☐ Six stems ivory velvet flocked grape leaves with three 1-inch (2.5 cm) leaves per stem
- ☐ Six ivory satin leaves 1¹/2 inches (4 cm) long
- ☐ 2 yards (1.8 m) ⁷/8-inch-wide (2 cm) ivory metallic lace-edged ribbon
- ☐ 2 yards (1.8 m) ¹/8-inch-wide (.3 cm) ivory satin gold-edged ribbon
- ☐ 2-ounce bunch glittered baby's breath
- ☐ 1¹/2-inch (4 cm) pin back
- ☐ Glue
- ☐ White floral tape
- ☐ 30-gauge cloth-covered wire
- ☐ One gold/ivory wedding bag, 8 inches (20 cm) × 10 inches (25.5 cm)

1. Floral tape together one rose, two stems flocked grape leaves, two satin leaves, two gold pearl sprays, two circular ivory pearl loops, and a small bunch of the glittered baby's breath. When taping, the leaves should be even with the rose head and the pearls should extend up to 1 inch (2.5 cm) longer than the rose.
2. Repeat step 1 to create two more clusters.
3. Floral tape two of the rose clusters together with one approximately 1 inch (2.5 cm) below the other one.
4. Leaving a 2-inch (5 cm) space, floral tape the third rose cluster in place. Overlap the stems of the clusters so the two clusters are positioned upward and the third rose cluster is angled downward.
5. With 2 yards (1.8 m) of the ivory metallic lace-edged ribbon and 2 yards (1.8 m) of the ¹/8-inch (.3 cm) ivory/gold ribbon, make a layered bow as directed on page 18. Each bow should have six 2-inch (5 cm) loops, one 6-inch streamer (15 cm), and one 9-inch (22.5 cm) streamer.
6. Attach the bow with wire, and glue it in the 2-inch (5 cm) space left between the rose cluster.
7. Glue the corsage to the pin back. Allow the corsage to dry, and attach to the wedding bag using the pin back.

Wedding Floral Design in Gift Bag

You will need:

- ☐ One wedding gift bag, 8 inches (20 cm) × 10 inches (25.5 cm)

- [ ] One 8-inch-tall (20 cm) white plastic vase with 4-inch-diameter (10 cm) opening
- [ ] Twelve 9-inch-long (22.5 cm) Boston fern leaves
- [ ] Two ivory silk hyacinths, floral portion measuring 6 inches (15 cm)
- [ ] Two ivory satin open roses with 3-inch (7.5 cm) flowers
- [ ] One stem ivory silk freesia, floral portion measuring 6 inches (15 cm)
- [ ] One stem ivory satin rosebuds with 1-inch (2.5 cm) heads
- [ ] Four stems ivory satin gardenias with 2-inch (5 cm) flowers
- [ ] Six ivory satin blossoms with 3-inch (7.5 cm) heads
- [ ] 2-ounce bunch glittered baby's breath
- [ ] 4 yards (3.6 m) 4-inch-wide (10 cm) tulle with metallic gold design
- [ ] 2$\frac{1}{3}$ yards (2.1 m) $\frac{5}{8}$-inch-wide (1.5 cm) wired ivory/gold satin ribbon
- [ ] Wooden floral picks

☐ White floral tape

☐ Glue

☐ Chenille stem

☐ Dry floral foam

☐ Spanish moss

☐ U-shaped pins

In creating this design imagine a loose L-shaped pattern.

1. Cut the foam to fit inside the vase. Allow the foam to extend 1 inch (2.5 cm) above the opening of the vase. Glue the foam into the vase.

2. Cover the foam with a small amount of Spanish moss. Secure the moss to the foam with the U-shaped pins. Insert the vase into the left side of the bag.

3. Position the hyacinths to the left on the top of the foam. One should extend 15 inches (38 cm) and the other 10 inches (25.5 cm) above the lip of the container. Cut the stems if necessary so that approximately 2 inches (5 cm) of each stem is inserted into the foam. Insert the stems into glue before inserting the flowers into the foam. These are the tallest flowers in the arrangement.

4. Position the freesia and the stem of five rosebuds to the right side on the center of the foam. These should extend 6 inches (15 cm) and 5 inches (12.5 cm), respectively, from the edge of the container. Cut the stems if necessary to achieve these lengths. Dip flowers into glue before inserting. These flowers create the bottom of the L pattern.

5. Add roses, gardenias, and 3-inch (7.5 cm) blossoms at varying heights to the front and side of the arrangement. Allow some flowers to be placed deeper into the arrangement. Do not have these flowers more than 10 inches (25.5 cm) above the lip of the container.

6. Fill in the front and sides of the arrangement with baby's breath.

7. Cut a 2-yard (5 cm) length of the ivory/metallic gold tulle. Make a four-loop bow with no center loop as directed on page 18. Each loop should measure 4 inches (10 cm). Secure with the chenille stem. Repeat to make a second bow.

8. Using the chenille stem securing each bow, position one bow at the lower left section of the design, near the lip of the container. Position the second bow to the lower back section of the arrangement to cover the foam and moss.

9. Randomly position the Boston fern leaves throughout the design filling space as needed.

10. Cut the ⁵⁄₈-inch (1.5 cm) wired ivory/gold satin ribbon into 24-inch-wide (60.5 cm) lengths. Make three ribbon loops of increasing size

with the ribbon, and attach to a wood pick as explained on page 13. Make a total of five triple-ribbon loops in this manner.

11. Use the triple-ribbon loops to fill in any open spaces within the design of the arrangement.

Bridal Bag with Haircomb

You will need:

☐ One gold/ivory wedding bag, 4¹/₂ inches (11.3 cm) × 6¹/₂ inches (16.3 cm)

☐ Four ivory satin rosebuds with 1-inch (2.5 cm) heads

☐ Two 3-inch (7.5 cm) ivory pearl sprays

☐ Four 3-inch (7.5 cm) gold pearl sprays

☐ Three 1¹/₄-inch (3.1 cm) gold lamé rose leaves

☐ Four stems ivory satin rose leaves with three 1-inch (2.5 cm) leaves per stem

☐ Six 2-inch (5 cm) ivory circular pearl stems

☐ 1-ounce bunch glittered baby's breath

☐ 1 yard (.9 m) ⁷/₈-inch-wide (2 cm) gold metallic lace-edged ribbon

☐ 3-inch (7.5 cm) clear plastic hair comb

☐ White floral tape

☐ Glue

☐ 30-gauge cloth-covered wire

The hairpiece is fashioned in the same manner as a corsage and glued to a plastic haircomb when finished.

1. Floral tape together one rose, one gold lamé leaf, one stem ivory satin leaves, two ivory pearl loops, a small amount of baby's breath and one gold pearl spray. Allow the leaves and pearl spray to extend 1 inch (2.5 cm) above the rosebud head.

2. Make two more clusters in the same manner.

3. Floral tape the three clusters together, making sure the rosebuds are at graduated positions as you floral tape them together into one group.

4. With the 1-yard (.9 m) length of $7/8$-inch (2 cm) ribbon, make a six-loop bow with a center loop as described on page 16. Loops should be $1^1/2$ inches (4 cm) long and streamers 6 inches (15 cm) long.

5. Attach the bow with the cloth-covered wire at the bottom of the flower cluster. Cut off excess wire, and floral tape over the ends of the wire to hide it.

6. Glue one rosebud and one stem ivory satin rose leaves in the space above the bow and underneath the bottom of the flower cluster.

7. Glue one gold pearl spray and two ivory pearl sprays to the top section of the flower cluster on the opposite end of the bow. Allow the pearl spray to extend 3 inches (7.5 cm) to 4 inches (10 cm) above the head of the top rosebud. Trim the end of the main stem to 1 inch (2.5 cm).

8. Glue the main stem of the flower cluster to the haircomb. Allow to dry.

Bridal Bag with Hairclip

You will need:

☐ Two ivory rosebuds with 1-inch (2.5 cm) heads

☐ One 3-inch (7.5 cm) barrette (French clip)

☐ One wedding bag, 3 inches (7.5 cm) × 4 inches (10 cm)

☐ Four stems ivory flocked grape leaves with three 1-inch (2.5 cm) leaves per stem

☐ Six $1^1/2$-inch (3.1 cm) gold lamé leaves

☐ Four 2-inch (5 cm) ivory circular pearl stems

☐ Two 3-inch (7.5 cm) ivory pearl sprays

☐ Four 3-inch (7.5 cm) gold pearl sprays

- ☐ Small amount glittered baby's breath
- ☐ One yard (.9 m) $^7/8$-inch-wide (2 cm) gold metallic lace-edged ribbon
- ☐ One yard (.9 m) $^1/8$-inch-wide (.3 cm) white double-faced satin ribbon with a gold edge
- ☐ Glue
- ☐ 30-gauge cloth-covered wire

1. After trimming the stems to $^1/2$ inch (1.3 cm), glue one stem of grape leaves to each end of the barrette facing in opposite directions. Extend the leaves 2 inches (5 cm) beyond the end of the barrette.

2. Remove the wires from three gold leaves. Glue these to the barrette positioning them just above the flocked grape leaves. Glue three more leaves to the other end of the barrette.

3. Glue one rosebud to each end of the barrette centering them between the three gold leaves at each end.

4. With one yard (.9 m) of the $^1/8$-inch-wide (.3 cm) and the $^7/8$-inch-wide (2 cm) ribbon, make a layered bow as directed on page 18. Each bow should have six $1^1/2$-inch (4 cm) loops with one 2-inch streamer (5 cm) and one 3-inch (7.5 cm) streamer. Glue this bow to the center of the barrette.

5. Glue two gold pearl sprays and one ivory pearl spray into the flowers at each end of the barrette. Allow the sprays to extend 4 inches (10 cm) beyond the end of the barrette. Glue the pearl sprays in the same manner to the opposite end of the barrette.

7. Glue three grape leaves into the loops of the bow to fill any empty spaces.

8. Glue a small amount of baby's breath to fill in any empty spaces.

Variation A very small barrette could be designed by simply gluing a tiny, multiloop bow using 2 yards (1.8 m) of 1/8-inch-wide (.3 cm) ribbon to a 2 1/2-inch-wide (6.5 cm) French clip. The bow should be about 2 inches (5 cm). After gluing the bow to the barrette, fill in each side with three flocked grape leaves, one pearl loop, and a tiny amount of glittered baby's breath.

VICTORIAN BOX

This box has a beauty all its own. By adding pearls and lace, you can enhance its Victorian look. See color photograph on page 87.

Beginner
1 hour
$17 – $20

You will need:

☐ Victorian-print box 8¹/₂ inches (21.3 cm) × 6¹/₂ inches (16.3 cm)

☐ 1 yard (.9 m) 8-inch (20 cm) ivory lace

☐ 1 yard (.9 m) 3-inch-wide (7.5 cm) mauve and ivory lace

☐ Two stems mauve satin daisies with six 1¹/₂-inch (4 cm) daisies per stem

☐ Twenty-four 1¹/₂-inch (4 cm) circular peach pearl stems

☐ Twelve stems pink/green leaves with three 1¹/₄-inch (3.1 cm) leaves per stem

☐ Glue

☐ 30-gauge cloth-covered wire

1. Cut three 12-inch (30.5 cm) lengths of the mauve/ivory lace. Make each length into a fan as directed on page 14. Set aside.

2. With one yard (.9 m) of the 8-inch (20 cm) lace, make a large four-loop bow with no center loop or streamers as directed on page 18. The loops should measure 4¹/₂ inches (11.3 cm) long.

3. Glue the large lace bow to the center of the box lid.

4. Randomly glue the three lace fans underneath and between the loops of the large lace bow, angling them upward.

5. Remove daisy heads from the main stem of the flower. Glue the 12 daisy heads and the 12 pink/green leaves randomly between the bow loops and lace fans.

6. Cut the stems of the 24 peach pearl loops to lengths of 1¹/₂ inches (4 cm). To finish the design, glue all the pearl loops randomly throughout the lace bow in the same manner as the daisies.

UMBRELLA SHOWER BAG

Simply decorated lace umbrellas give this shower gift bag a professionally gift-wrapped look (see illustration on next page). The umbrellas could be color-coordinated to the color scheme of the wedding party. Ours are coordinated to the colors found on the gift bag itself. See color photograph on page 92.

You will need:

☐ One gift bag with umbrella design, 8¹/₂ inches (21.3 cm) × 4¹/₂ inches (11.3 cm) diameter × 11 inches (28 cm) tall

☐ Two 6-inch (15 cm) lace umbrellas

☐ Coral spray paint

☐ Twelve ³/₄-inch (1.8 cm) purple satin ribbon roses with leaves

Intermediate
I hour
$22 – $25

☐ Twelve ¹/₂-inch (1.3 cm) peach satin ribbon roses with leaves

☐ 4 yards (3.6 m) ¹/₄-inch-wide (.6 cm) ivory satin picot-edged ribbon

☐ 2 yards (1.8 m) ¹/₄-inch-wide (.6 cm) coral satin picot-edged ribbon

☐ 2 yards (1.8 m) ¹/₈-inch-wide (.3 cm) purple satin ribbon

☐ 2 yards (1.8 m) 6-inch-wide (15 cm) aqua/gold flecked tulle

☐ White chenille stem

☐ Glue

☐ 30-gauge cloth-covered wire

1. Cut the ivory picot-edged ribbon into 24 6-inch (15 cm) lengths. Make 24 simple two-loop bows (just like you tie a shoelace). Set aside.

2. Spray the two lace umbrellas with coral spray paint. Allow to dry.

3. Glue one bow to each spoke of the umbrella, about ¹/₂ inch (1.3 cm) from the top edge. Our umbrellas had eight spokes each. Glue four bows around the top center of the umbrella. Glue 12 bows on the other umbrella in the same manner.

4. Glue the purple satin ribbon roses alternately with the peach satin ribbon roses to the center of each ivory bow.

5. Using the 2-yard (1.8 m) length of the aqua/gold tulle, make a six-loop bow with 6-inch-long (15 cm) streamers as directed on page 16. The loops should measure 4 inches (10 cm) long. Set aside.

6. Make a 14-loop bow with 4-inch (10 cm) streamers using the coral picot-edged ribbon. Repeat with the purple satin ribbon.

7. Secure the three bows together as when forming a layered bow, explained on page 18.

8. Secure the handles of the two umbrellas together with cloth-covered wire.

9. Glue the layered bow at the spot where the umbrella handles meet.

10. Near the top of the bag, insert a chenille stem from the outside. At a point 2 inches (5 cm) away, bring the end of the chenille stem back out through the bag. The two ends of the chenille stem should be extending from the outside of the bag.

11. Wrap the chenille stem around the umbrella handles to secure them to the bag.

LOVE BAG GROUPING

The ribbon treatment and embellishments used in this design create a colorful and elegantly romantic effect for these gift bags. Fill with bath oils, massage creams, etc., to continue the theme of romance. See color photograph on page 87.

Intermediate
2 hours (whole grouping)
Large gift bag:
$15 – $18
Medium gift bag:
$8 – $10
Small gift bag:
$5 – $8

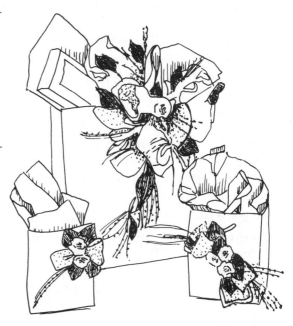

Large Gift Bag

You will need:

- ☐ One gift bag, 7^1/2 inches wide (18.8 cm) × 4^1/2 inches deep (11.3 cm) × 10 inches (25.5 cm) tall
- ☐ 2 yards (1.8 m) 2^1/2-inch-wide (6.5 cm) mauve sheer ribbon
- ☐ 1^1/2 yards (1.3 m) 2^1/2-inch-wide (6.5 cm) white lace ribbon
- ☐ Seventeen raspberry-colored 3 mm pearl sprays
- ☐ Fifteen 1^1/2-inch (4 cm) cranberry satin leaves

1. Make a layered bow with 1^1/2 yards (1.3 m) each of the sheer mauve ribbon and the white lace ribbon, as directed on page 18. The loops should each measure 4 inches (10 cm).
2. Trim the stems to ^{1}/2 inch (1.3 cm) and randomly glue the 15 cranberry leaves throughout the bow loops. Allow some to drape down from the bow.
3. Randomly glue the 17 raspberry pearl sprays throughout the bow loops in the same manner that the leaves were glued. Secure the bow to the bag with the chenille stem of the bow.

Medium Gift Bag

You will need:

- ☐ One gift bag, 4 inches wide (10 cm) × 2^1/2 inches (6.5 cm) deep × 5 inches (12.5 cm) tall
- ☐ ^{1}/3 yard (30.5 cm) 2^1/2-inch-wide (6.5 cm) mauve sheer ribbon
- ☐ ^{1}/2 yard (.5 m) 1^3/8-inch-wide (3.4 cm) mauve lace-edged ribbon
- ☐ Three 1-inch (2.5 cm) pink ribbon roses
- ☐ Six 1^1/2-inch (4 cm) cranberry satin leaves
- ☐ Four 3 mm raspberry pearl sprays

1. Using the mauve sheer ribbon, make a two-loop bow with no center loop, as directed on page 18. Set aside.
2. With the 1^3/8-inch (3.4 cm) mauve lace-edged ribbon, make a four-loop bow with no center loop as directed on page 18.
3. Glue the bow made in step 2 on top of the bow made in step 1.
4. Glue two raspberry pearl sprays between the ribbon loops on each side of the bow. Allow the sprays to extend 3 inches (7.5 cm) beyond the bow.
5. Glue three ribbon roses to the center of the bow created.

6. Glue six cranberry leaves between the ribbon loops of the bow.

7. Glue the bow to the bag.

Small Gift Bag

You will need:

- ☐ One gift bag, 3½ inches (8.8 cm) wide × 1½ inches (4 cm) deep × 4½ inches (11.3 cm) tall
- ☐ 1 yard (.9 m) ⅝-inch-wide (1.5 cm) sheer mauve ribbon
- ☐ Two 1-inch (2.5 cm) pink ribbon roses
- ☐ Three 1½-inch (4 cm) cranberry satin leaves
- ☐ Three 3 mm raspberry pearl sprays
- ☐ 30-gauge cloth-covered wire
- ☐ Glue

1. Make an eight-loop bow with the ⅝-inch (1.5 cm) sheer mauve ribbon. Each loop should measure 1½ inches (4 cm) long with no center loop.

2. Glue three cranberry leaves to the back of the bow.

3. Glue two ribbon roses to the center of the bow. Cut the stem very short.

4. Add two raspberry pearl sprays to each side of the bow. Cut to desired length. Allow these to extend 3 inches (7.5 cm) beyond the bow.

5. Glue the bow to the bag.

CHAPTER 5

Holiday Designs

*N*umerous opportunities arise throughout the year to create special gift baskets, bags, and boxes for friends and family. This chapter will give you many wonderful ideas to get you started on your way. Don't forget to use your imagination to adapt these designs to suit your own needs.

ABACA HEART BASKET WITH LID

Beginner
30 minutes
$13 – $15

This abaca heart basket is pretty even without decorations. Add bright red pearls, lace, and Valentine decorations for a romantic look. See color photograph on page 88.

You will need:

☐ One 9-inch (22.5 cm) abaca heart basket with lid

☐ 2/3 yard (.6 m) 1 1/2-inch-wide (4 cm) white gathered lace

☐ 2/3 yard (.6 m) 8 mm fused red beads

☐ 1 1/2 yards (1.3 m) 1-inch-wide (2.5 cm) red satin lace-edged ribbon

☐ Four 1-inch (2.5 cm) Valentine heart picks

☐ 1 yard (.9 m) 1-inch-wide (2.5 cm) cutout heart ribbon (ours says "I Love You").

☐ Glue

☐ 30-gauge white cloth-covered wire

☐ One sheet red tissue paper

1. Glue the gathered lace around the top edge of the base of the basket. Glue the beads on top of the lace.

2. Make a six-loop bow with the lace-edged ribbon as directed on page 16. This bow should not have a center loop.

3. Make a four-loop bow with the red heart cutout ribbon.

4. Secure the two bows together to form a layered bow, as explained on page 18. Glue the bow to the top center of the basket lid.

5. Glue the Valentine picks around the loops of the bow.

6. Use a sheet of red tissue paper to fill the basket before adding gifts or candies.

VALENTINE BOX WITH TEDDY BEAR

The Valentine gift box pictured on the next page is a quick gift idea for a friend or relative. Add an embellished bow to dress up the outside, and include a small stuffed bear with the treats inside the box. See color photograph on page 88.

You will need:

☐ One Valentine box with handles, 5 inches (12.5 cm) × 8 inches (20 cm)

☐ 1 yard (.9 m) 5/8-inch-wide (1.5 cm) Valentine ribbon

☐ One 2-inch (5 cm) flocked bear

☐ One 4-inch (10 cm) stuffed bear

Beginner
20 minutes
$5 – $7

☐ Glue

☐ 30-gauge cloth-covered wire

1. Make a six-loop bow with no center loop as directed on page 18. Loops should measure 2¹/₂ inches (6.5 cm) long with two 3-inch (7.5 cm) streamers.

2. Glue the 2-inch (5 cm) flocked bear to the center of the bow.

3. Attach the bow with the cloth-covered wire to the handle of the box.

MYLAR HEART BAG

Mylar bags make gift wrapping easy. Just pop your gift inside and tie the bag shut. Creative bow treatment gives your gift the finishing touch. See color photograph on page 90.

You will need:

☐ One mylar bag with heart decorations, 9 inches (22.5 cm) × 12 inches (30.5 cm)

☐ 1¹/₃ yard (1.2 m) 2-inch-wide (5 cm) multicolor mum bow ribbon

☐ Two 1¹/₄-inch (3.1 cm) lacquered heart picks

☐ Glue

☐ Rubber band

1. Fill bag with gift items.

2. Close bag by pinching the top together. Wrap with the rubber band. Pull ends of 1-yard (.9 m) mum bow ribbon to gather together tightly.

Wrap the gathered ribbon around the top of the bag and tie the ends together to secure. Trim away excess ribbon ends.

3. Pull the threads of the remaining length of mum bow ribbon to form a tight mum flower. Tie ends to secure flower. Trim away excess ends. Glue this flower into the inside of the open part of the bag.

4. Cut the stems of the heart picks to a length of 2 inches (5 cm). Glue the stems inside the mum extending about 1 inch (2.5 cm) above the flower.

ST. PATRICK'S DAY SHAMROCK BAG

This bag would be a pleasant surprise for an Irish friend. But then again, aren't we all Irish on St. Patrick's Day? This bag is a perfect size to hold some homemade Irish soda bread or another treat of your choice. See color photograph on page 88.

You will need:

☐ One green-and-white-striped paper bag, 5¹/₂ inches (13.8 cm) × 1 inch (2.5 cm)

☐ Three white silk carnations

☐ One 9-inch (22.5 cm) paper shamrock

☐ 1 yard (.9 m) 3-inch-wide (7.5 cm) green metallic striped ribbon

Beginner
I hour
$7 – $9

☐ Three ivy stems, each stem 4 inches (10 cm) long

☐ Three paper shamrock picks

☐ 2 yards (1.8 m) ³/₈-inch-wide (.9 cm) white curling ribbon

☐ 2 yards (1.8 m) ¹/₈-inch-wide (.3 cm) metallic green curling ribbon

☐ 30-gauge cloth-covered wire

☐ Glue

☐ Green floral tape

1. Fill bag with gift items. Fold down 1¹/₂ inches (4 cm) of the top of the bag and staple it shut.

2. Glue the 9-inch (22.5 cm) shamrock to the front of the bag. Allow the shamrock to extend 3 inches (7.5 cm) above the fold of the bag.

3. Cut the stems of the carnations to a length of 3 inches (7.5 cm).

4. Floral tape one stem of ivy to one carnation. Allow three leaves of ivy to extend above the carnation head. Repeat with the other two ivy stems and carnations.

5. Floral tape the three carnations with ivy stems attached together in a cluster. Allow one carnation to extend 2 inches (5 cm) above the other two. Two of the carnations may be at the same level. Glue this cluster to the center of the paper shamrock.

6. Make a four-loop tailored bow with 1 yard (.9 m) of the 3-inch (7.5 cm) metallic ribbon as directed on page 20. The bow should measure 7 inches (17.5 cm) across. Glue this bow to the paper shamrock to cover the stems of the flower cluster.

7. Cut the stems of three shamrock picks to a length of 2 inches (5 cm). Randomly glue the picks into the flower cluster.

8. Cut eight lengths of green curling ribbon, each length measuring 12 inches (30.5 cm). Cut four lengths of the white curling ribbon, each length measuring 18 inches (45.5 cm).

9. Gather all the cut pieces of ribbon together. Secure around the center of this cluster of ribbon with a 6-inch length (15 cm) of cloth-covered wire to form one large cluster of ribbon streamers. Curl the ends of the ribbons with the blade of a pair of scissors.

10. Glue this ribbon cluster into the space between the carnations on the paper shamrock.

SPRING GIFT BASKET

Welcome spring with this colorful gift basket. Dogwood blossoms, blue jays, and ribbon streamers combine to create a lovely springtime feeling. See color photograph on page 89.

Advanced
2 hours
$20 – $25

You will need:

- ☐ One 14-inch (35 cm) round basket, 20 inches tall (50.5 cm) × 10 inches (25.5 cm) deep
- ☐ 2 ounces green-dyed Spanish moss
- ☐ Six stems 6-inch (15 cm) pink dogwood, each stem having three 2½-inch (6.5 cm) flowers
- ☐ One 3-inch (7.5 cm) bird's nest
- ☐ Six 1-inch (2.5 cm) plastic bird eggs in assorted colors
- ☐ Two 5-inch (12.5 cm) feathered blue jays
- ☐ Eight 1-inch (2.5 cm) blue silk flower blossoms
- ☐ One stem yellow silk double blossoms, containing six sections of four ½-inch (1.3 cm) flowers per section
- ☐ 2½ yards (2.3 m) ½-inch-wide (1.3 cm) deep-purple satin picot-edged ribbon
- ☐ 2½ yards (2.3 m) ½ inch-wide (1.3 cm) light-pink satin picot-edged ribbon
- ☐ 2½ yards (2.3 m) ½-inch-wide (1.3 cm) light-blue satin picot-edged ribbon
- ☐ 2½ yards (2.3 m) ⅛-inch-wide (.3 cm) yellow double-faced satin ribbon
- ☐ 2½ yards (2.3 m) ⅛-inch-wide (.3 cm) aqua double-faced satin ribbon
- ☐ Glue
- ☐ 30-gauge cloth-covered wire

1. Glue Spanish moss at the base of one side of the basket handle. With the handle as the center point, cover an area about 14 inches (35 cm) long along the top edge of the basket.

2. Cut a 1-yard (.9 m) length of the deep-purple satin ribbon. Cut a 1-yard (.9 m) length of the light-pink satin ribbon. Glue the ends of these two ribbon lengths near the base of the basket handle covered with Spanish moss. Drape and loop the ribbon up and around the basket handle. Loosely tie the ribbons together where they end at a point on the basket handle. Allow 6 inches (15 cm) to 8 inches (20 cm) of the ribbon to drape down from the handle.

3. Using 1½ of each of the five ribbons, make a layered bow following instructions on page 18. Ribbon loops should measure about 2½ inches (6.5 cm) and streamers may vary from 6 inches (15 cm) to 8 inches (20 cm).

4. Glue this bow into the Spanish moss at the right side of the base of the basket handle.

5. Glue the eggs into the nest. Glue the nest to the top edge of the basket at the left side of the handle, about 2 inches (5 cm) away from the bow.

6. Glue two stems of pink dogwood blossoms to the top edge of the basket near the bird's nest. Glue two more stems into the area near the bow.

7. Glue two stems of the dogwood blossoms to the basket handle angling them upward. The last flower should be positioned about 10 inches (25.5 cm) away from the bow at the heart of the design.

8. Randomly glue the 1-inch (2.5 cm) blue silk flower blossoms and the $1/2$-inch (1.3 cm) yellow silk blossoms throughout the design on the edge of the basket and along the basket handle.

9. Glue one blue jay about 6 inches (15 cm) to the left of the basket handle next to the bird's nest.

10. Glue the other blue jay at a point near the tip of the tallest dogwood blossom, about 12 inches (30.5 cm) up the handle from the basket edge.

11. Use the remaining 1-yard (.9 m) lengths of the ribbons to drape from each blue jay to the bow area.

12. Glue the ribbon ends to the beaks of each blue jay, allowing 8 inches (20 cm) to 10 inches (25.5 cm) of the ribbon to drape down. Drape the ribbon throughout the design. Glue at random points to secure the ribbon.

SPRINGTIME EASTER BASKET

Three simple elements combine to create this simple Easter basket. The design is centered at the top of the basket handle, leaving more room in the basket for Easter goodies. See color photograph on page 88.

You will need:

☐ One blue oval basket, 6 inches (15 cm) × 8 inches (20 cm) diameter × 9 inches (22.5 cm) tall × 3 inches (7.5 cm) deep

☐ One 3-inch (7.5 cm) purple/blue feathered bird

☐ Six $3/4$-inch (1.8 cm) plastic robin eggs

☐ 3 yards (2.7 m) $1/4$-inch-wide (.6 cm) aqua curling ribbon

☐ 3 yards (2.7 m) $1/4$-inch-wide (.6 cm) pink curling ribbon

☐ 3 yards (2.7 m) $1/4$-inch-wide (.6 cm) bright yellow curling ribbon

☐ 3 yards (2.7 m) $1/4$-inch-wide (.6 cm) metallic blue curling ribbon

☐ 30-gauge cloth-covered wire

☐ Glue

Beginner
30 minutes
$9 – $11

1. Using the 3-yard lengths of all four ribbons, make a layered bow following the instructions on page 18. The loops should measure 2½ inches (6.5 cm), and the streamers should be 12 inches (30.5 cm) to 15 inches (38 cm) long before curling.

2. Glue the bow to the top center of the basket handle. Curl the ribbon ends with the blade of a pair of scissors.

3. Glue the bird to the center of the bow at the top of the handle.

4. Glue three eggs on each side of the bow.

TWO-TIERED EASTER BASKET

Create an unusual decorative effect by stacking a smaller look-alike basket on top of a larger one. Add flowers and ribbon before filling with candies or gift items. See color photograph on page 88.

You will need:

☐ One oval pink basket, 5 inches (12.5 cm) × 6 inches (15 cm) diameter × 8 inches (20 cm) high × 3 inches (7.5 cm) deep

Intermediate
45 minutes
$15 – $18

- ☐ One oval pink basket, 4 inches (10 cm) × 5 inches (12.5 cm) diameter × 7 inches (17.5 cm) high × 2 inches (5 cm) deep
- ☐ Two blocks dry floral foam, 2 inches (5 cm) × 3 inches (5.7 cm) × 2 inches (5 cm)
- ☐ 1 ounce green Easter grass
- ☐ 1 yard (.9 m) $^5/_8$-inch-wide (1.5 cm) yellow iridescent ribbon
- ☐ 3 yards (2.7 m) $^3/_8$-inch-wide (.9 cm) lavender iridescent ribbon
- ☐ One 4-inch (10 cm) white open rose
- ☐ One 1-inch (2.5 cm) white rosebud
- ☐ Six 2-inch (5 cm) white alstroemeria flowers
- ☐ Two 1$^1/_2$-inch (4 cm) flocked bunnies on a wire pick (one blue and one yellow)
- ☐ Glue

☐ 30-gauge cloth-covered wire

☐ Five wood picks

☐ U-shaped craft pins

1. Glue one block of foam into each of the baskets. Cover the foam with Easter grass, and secure the grass with U-shaped pins.

2. Cut the 1-yard (.9 m) length of the yellow iridescent ribbon into six 6-inch (15 cm) lengths. Make a ribbon loop with each piece following instructions on page 13. Attach each loop to a wooden pick.

3. Repeat step 2 with the lavender iridescent ribbon.

4. With 2 yards (1.8 m) of the lavender iridescent ribbon, make a twenty-loop bow as directed on page 16. The loops should measure 2^1/2 inches (6.5 cm) and have 5-inch (12.5 cm) streamers.

5. Glue the smaller basket to the top edge of the right side of the larger basket. The baskets are glued in opposite directions: The larger one has its long side facing the viewer, and the smaller one has its narrow side facing the viewer.

6. Casually arrange the flowers to fill the smaller basket. Position the open rose to face the viewer. The flowers should extend in various lengths from 2 inches (5 cm) to 8 inches (20 cm) above the rim of the basket. Place the larger flowers near the base of the design with the smaller ones extending further away. Trim the stems of the flowers if necessary.

7. Position the twenty-loop lavender bow deep into the design to fill any space not covered with flowers.

8. Fill the bottom basket with the yellow and lavender ribbon loops.

9. Cut the stem of the wood pick on the blue flocked bunny to a length of 5 inches (12.5 cm). Insert it into the foam of the smaller basket in between the flowers. Cut the stem of the yellow flocked bunny to a length of 3 inches (7.5 cm). Insert it into the foam of the larger basket between the ribbon loops.

MOTHER'S DAY SEWING BASKET

What a nice surprise for Mom! Ribbon, silk flowers, and a pretty wired bead garland decorate this basket. Fill the basket with gift items related to her hobby or favorite pastimes. See color photograph on page 93.

You will need:

☐ One rectangular basket, 8 inches (20 cm) × 12 inches diameter (30.5 cm) × 14 inches (35 cm) tall × 5 inches (12.5 cm) deep

☐ Pink spray webbing

☐ Purple spray webbing

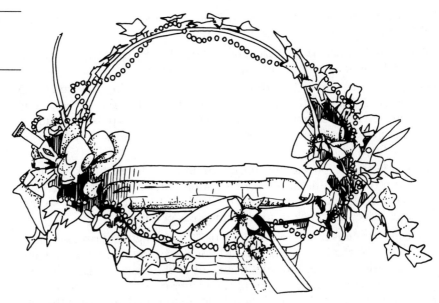

Advanced
1½ hours
$27 – $30

- ☐ Twelve 2-inch (5 cm) yellow tiger lilies
- ☐ Four 1½-inch (4 cm) yellow tiger lily buds
- ☐ Ten 1-inch (2.5 cm) lavender rosebuds
- ☐ One stem English ivy with twelve 6-inch (15 cm) sections, each containing seven leaves
- ☐ 3½ yards (3.2 m) 3-inch-wide (7.5 cm) flocked purple/pink polka dot tulle
- ☐ 3½ yards (3.2 m) 1⅜-inch-wide (3.4 cm) lavender floral ribbon
- ☐ Two blocks dry floral foam, 2 inches (5 cm) × 3 inches (7.5 cm) × 2 inches (5 cm)
- ☐ 1 ounce Spanish moss
- ☐ 36 U-shaped pins
- ☐ Green floral tape
- ☐ 30-gauge cloth-covered wire
- ☐ 20-gauge stem wire
- ☐ Four wooden picks with sewing theme: ruler, spool, scissors, and iron
- ☐ 2 yards (1.8 m) ¼-inch-wide (.6 cm) wired purple bead garland
- ☐ Glue

1. Spray basket with pink and purple webbing. (The more you spray, the fuller the webbing will appear.) Allow the webbing to dry.

2. Glue one block of floral foam to the base of each side of the basket handle. Hold in place until secure.

3. Cover each block of foam with Spanish moss. Insert U-shaped pins through the moss and into the foam to secure.

4. Cut an 18-inch (45.5 cm) length of the polka dot tulle and an 18-inch (45.5 cm) length of the lavender ribbon. Set aside.

5. Cut the remaining 3 yards (2.7 m) of the polka dot tulle and the 3 yards (2.7 m) of the lavender floral ribbon into 6-inch (30.5 cm) lengths. Make eighteen ribbon-loop picks with the polka dot tulle as directed on page 13. Make eighteen ribbon-loop picks with the lavender floral ribbon.

6. Use U-shaped pins to attach the ribbon loops to the blocks of floral foam on each side of the basket handle. Attach eight loops of each type of ribbon to each side of the basket. Arrange the loops so that they cover the block of foam as much as possible.

7. Glue the ends of the two 18-inch (45.5 cm) lengths of ribbon (cut in step 4) to the base of the left side of the basket handle. Drape and loop the ribbon around the front rim of the basket. Attach the two ribbons at a point just right of the center on the side of the basket. Allow about 7 inches (17.5 cm) of the ribbons to drape down the side of the basket.

8. If the stems of the lilies are not firm, floral tape a 2-inch length of 20-gauge wire to each flower stem.

9. Randomly position five 2-inch (5 cm) lilies and two 1½-inch (4 cm) buds into the ribbon-loop cluster on one side of the basket. Repeat, adding the same amount of lilies and buds to the opposite side of the basket.

10. Randomly place four lavender rosebuds, in the same manner as the lilies, into the floral foam between the ribbon loops on each side of the basket handle.

11. Glue a lily and rosebud to the left front corner of the basket edge. Glue a lily and rosebud to the basket edge to the right of center on the side of the basket.

12. Randomly glue the 6-inch (15 cm) ivy branches into the ribbon-loop clusters, around the front basket edge and up over the basket handle.

13. Secure one end of the pearl garland with glue at the base of one side of the basket handle. Drape and loop the pearls around the basket handle and across the front edge of the basket. Secure the end of the pearls at the point where they were first attached.

14. Cut the stems of the four wooden sewing picks to a length of 2 inches (5 cm). Position two picks into the floral foam on each side of the basket handle.

HALLOWEEN BAG

Deliver your Halloween treats in this humorous dancing-skeleton bag. Our embellished bow completes the spooky Halloween effect. See color photograph on page 94.

Beginner
30 minutes
$8 – $10

You will need:

□ Skeleton gift bag, 8¹/₂ inches (21.3 cm) × 10 inches (25.5 cm)
□ 1-ounce bag of spider webbing
□ 1 yard (.9 m) 1¹/₂-inch-wide (4 cm) black mesh ribbon
□ 1 yard (.9 m) 2-inch-wide (5 cm) orange satin wired ribbon
□ Two 1¹/₂-inch (4 cm) flocked skulls
□ Three 1-inch (2.5 cm) black plastic spiders
□ 30-gauge cloth-covered wire
□ Glue

1. Make a layered bow with the black mesh and the orange satin ribbon as directed on page 18. The orange bow should have four loops 3 inches (7.5 cm) long with two 4-inch (10 cm) streamers and no center

loop. The black bow should have six 2^1/$_2$-inch-long (6.5 cm) loops with two 4-inch (10 cm) streamers.

2. Glue the two flocked skulls to the center of the layered bow.

3. Spread the spider webbing out, and glue it to the back of the bow.

4. Glue the three plastic spiders randomly to the streamers and the bow loops.

5. Glue the bow to the top left front corner of the bag.

SPOOKY HALLOWEEN TREAT BASKET

Those with a fear of spiders might not want to put their hand in this basket for a treat! It would make a fun centerpiece for a kids' or grown-ups' Halloween party. See color photograph on page 94.

Intermediate
1 hour
$25 – $28

You will need:

☐ One round basket, 12 inches (30.5 cm) diameter × 6 inches (15 cm) deep × 15 inches (39 cm) tall

☐ Orange spray paint

☐ Black spray paint

☐ 1-ounce bunch baby eucalyptus

☐ 2-ounce bunch preserved baby's breath

☐ 2-ounce package sphagnum moss

☐ Six 3-inch (7.5 cm) silk fall leaves

☐ 2 yards (1.8 m) 2-inch-wide (5 cm) orange wired ribbon

☐ One 1$\frac{1}{2}$-inch (4 cm) white flocked skull

☐ Two 3-inch (7.5 cm) flocked bats

☐ Two 4-inch (10 cm) large hairy spiders

☐ One small package spider webbing

☐ Five 2-inch (5 cm) plastic spiders

☐ Glue

☐ 30-gauge cloth-covered wire

1. Spray basket with orange spray paint. Allow to dry.

2. Using short, quick bursts, spray black paint on the basket. Do not cover it completely.

3. Cut the eucalyptus into eight 4-inch (10 cm) pieces. Spray paint these pieces with black paint. Allow to dry. Set aside.

4. Make an eight-loop bow with the orange wired ribbon as directed on page 16. Loops should measure 3 inches (7.5 cm) long and have two 4-inch (10 cm) streamers with no center loop.

5. Glue pieces of the moss to the edge of the basket. Start at the base of one side of the basket handle. Cover about a 12-inch-long (30.5 cm) section of the basket edge, 6 inches (15 cm) on each side of the handle.

6. Glue the wired bow to the center of the mossed area at the base of the handle.

7. Glue three silk fall leaves to the basket edge at each side of the bow. Allow them to slightly overlap one another.

8. Glue four of the eucalyptus pieces to the basket edge at the side of the area around the bow.

9. Glue 2-inch (5 cm) bunches of baby's breath in between the fall leaves and eucalyptus.

10. Drape and glue the spider webbing around the basket edge and handle.

11. Glue spiders and bats randomly around the basket edge and handle to complete the Halloween effect.

12. Glue the white flocked skull to the center of the bow. (This will be used in place of a center loop.)

"GIFT FROM SANTA" BASKET

Colorful ribbon and a simple cluster of Christmas greens and berries are all the decorations this basket needs. Fill with shiny foil paper and gift items to complete the design. See color photograph on page 89.

Beginner
30 minutes
$14 – $16

You will need:

☐ One oval basket, 8 inches (20 cm) × 14 inches (35 cm) diameter × 12 inches (30.5 cm) tall × 6 inches (15 cm) deep

☐ 2 yards (1.8 m) 1½ inch wide (4 cm) red satin ribbon screen-printed with "A Gift from Santa"

☐ Two 6-inch pine picks with four 3-inch (7.5 cm) sections per pick

☐ One 4-inch (10 cm) holly cluster

☐ One 4-inch (10 cm) red/gold candy cane

☐ Glue

☐ 30-gauge cloth-covered wire

1. Cut the stems of the two pine picks to a length of 1 inch (2.5 cm). Glue these two picks in opposite directions, end to end, slightly overlapping one another on the side of the basket handle. The pine cluster should measure about 15 inches (38 cm) from tip to tip.

2. Make an eight-loop tailored bow with the screen-printed ribbon as

directed on page 20. One streamer should measure 6 inches (15 cm), and the other streamer 18 inches (45.5 cm). The loops should measure 3 inches (7.5 cm), 3^1/$_2$ inches (8.8 cm), 4 inches (10 cm), and 4^1/$_2$ inches (11.3 cm).

3. Glue the bow to the center of the pine cluster with the short streamer angling down and the long streamer angling up.

4. Loosely drape and loop the 18-inch-long (45.5 cm) streamer up and over the basket handle to the other side of the basket. Glue the ribbon at two points along the handle, and allow it to drape down the back side of the basket.

5. Cut the stem of the holly cluster to a length of 1 inch (2.5 cm). Glue to the basket handle behind the bow, near the center.

6. Glue the candy cane to the basket handle just above the holly cluster. Allow it to angle away from the handle.

CHRISTMAS CANDY BOX

This project couldn't be any simpler: Just glue prepainted wood pieces to this box for a quick holiday decoration. It would be a perfect gift for the kids to give grandma and grandpa for Christmas.

The design of your basket will depend on the wood pieces available to you. Create little scenes to decorate the sides of the basket. See color photograph on page 89.

Beginner
10 minutes
$7 – $9

You will need:

☐ One rectangular box with lid, 3 inches (7.5 cm) × 5 inches (12.5 cm)
☐ Nine 1¹/₂-inch (4 cm) prepainted Christmas trees
☐ Three 2-inch (5 cm) prepainted wood houses
☐ One 1¹/₂-inch (4 cm) prepainted wood house
☐ Glue

1. Glue one 2-inch (5 cm) house and two 1¹/₂-inch (4 cm) Christmas trees to the top of the basket lid. Glue the house to the center of the lid and one tree on each side of it.
2. Glue a house to the front panel of the basket with a tree on each side of the house.
3. Glue two trees on each side of the basket.
4. Glue a Christmas tree to the center of the back side of the basket. Glue a house on each side of the tree.

HAPPY HOLIDAY GIFT BASKET

The basket on the next page is pretty just by itself. Add a little bit of ribbon, some shiny red berries, and Christmas greens to give it that little something extra. It would make a charming table centerpiece filled with holiday candies or potpourri. See color photograph on page 89.

Beginner
I hour
$18 – $20

You will need:

- [ ] One oval red and white holiday basket with window and shutters, 7 inches (17.5 cm) × 8 inches (20 cm) diameter × 15 inches (38 cm) tall × 8 inches (20 cm) deep
- [ ] One stem glittered pine with twelve 4-inch (10 cm) sections
- [ ] One stem gold-glittered cedar spray with six 4-inch (10 cm) sections
- [ ] One stem glittered white cedar with eight 3-inch (7.5 cm) sections
- [ ] One shiny red berry spray with 10 branches of five berries per branch
- [ ] 1 yard (.9 m) 1-inch-wide (2.5 cm) red and green plaid ribbon
- [ ] Glue
- [ ] 32-gauge cloth-covered wire

1. Make a four-loop bow with 3-inch-long (7.5 cm) loops as directed on page 16. Set aside.
2. Pull the 12 sections off the main stem of the glittered pine stem. Glue these pieces section by section in a loose L pattern along the left side of the basket and up the handle.
3. Pull the six sections off the main stem of the gold-glittered cedar stem. Glue these to fill in the pattern formed by the pine pieces.
4. Pull the eight sections off the main stem of the glittered white cedar stem. Glue these pieces evenly throughout the design.
5. Cut the berry spray into 10 separate sections. Individually glue these throughout the design.
6. Glue the bow made in step 1 to the center section of the design.

CHRISTMAS BASKET

Advanced
2 hours
$26 – $30

This basket has been given an elegant look by adding gold glass balls and fans. Simple techniques are used to create this design. The illustration on the left is the front of the design and the one on the right is the back view. See color photograph on page 89.

You will need:

☐ One round basket, 12 inches (30.5 cm) diameter × 16 inches (40.5 cm) tall × 7 inches (17.5 cm) deep

☐ 1¹/₂ yards (1.3 m) 6-inch-wide (15 cm) white gathered lace

☐ 2 yards (1.8 m) 5 mm fused pearls

☐ 2 yards (1.8 m) ¹/₄-inch-wide (.6 cm) gold lamé tubing

☐ 2 yards (1.8 m) ¹/₄-inch-wide (.6 cm) red/green/gold plaid tubing

☐ Six flocked plastic pine picks with seven sections per stem

☐ Twelve red satin rosebuds with 1-inch (2.5 cm) heads

☐ Three 1¹/₄-inch (3.1 cm) gold glass balls

☐ Two Christmas picks with a pine cone, package, and lamé ball on each

☐ Two 4-inch (10 cm) gold foil fans

☐ Six white 3 mm pearl sprays

☐ ¹/₂ yard (.5 m) 3-inch-wide (7.5 cm) gold net ribbon

☐ Glue

☐ 30-gauge cloth-covered wire

1. Starting at the base of one side of the basket handle, glue the 1¹/₂-yard length (1.3 m) of gathered lace around the outside edge of the basket. Allow 1 inch (2.5 cm) of the lace to extend above the lip of the basket.

2. With 2 yards (1.8 m) each of the fused pearls, gold lamé tubing, and plaid tubing, make a braid as directed on page 15. Glue this braid on top of the lace attached to the basket. There should be 4 inches (10 cm) of lace draping below the braid and 1 inch (2.5 cm) extending above the braid.

3. At the base of the handle on one side of the basket, glue three of the plastic pine picks in a triangle pattern.

4. Cut the stem of the pine-cone-and-package pick to a length of 1 inch (2.5 cm). Glue this pick to the center bottom of the triangle formed by the three pine picks.

5. Cut the stem of one more pine pick to a length of 1 inch (2.5 cm) and glue it, angled upward, just above the pine-cone-and-package pick. This should fill in the space between the package pick and the tallest pine pick.

Step 3

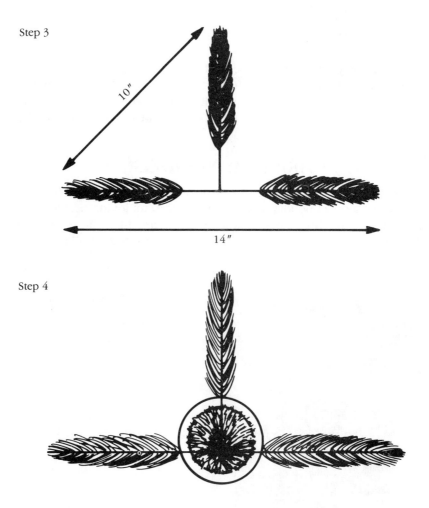

Step 4

6. Glue one gold fan to each side of the pine-cone-and-package pick. Angle them in opposite directions—one up, one down.

7. Cut the rosebuds from the main stem of the flower, leaving a 1-inch (2.5 cm) stem on each bud. Glue the rosebuds randomly throughout the pine picks.

8. Cut the stems of the pearl sprays to a $1/2$-inch (1.3 cm) length. Randomly glue the pearl sprays throughout the design.

9. Cut the stems of the glass balls to a 1-inch (2.5 cm) length. Glue them in a decorative fashion within the design created.

10. On the opposite side of the basket handle, glue two pine picks horizontally along the edge of the basket. Cut the stems of the pine picks to a length of 1 inch (2.5 cm). The pine picks should measure 11 inches (28 cm) from tip to tip.

11. Glue the last pine-cone-and-package pick to the center of the pine picks.

12. Cut the ½ yard (.5 m) gold net ribbon into two equal pieces. Make two single-ribbon loops as directed on page 13. The loops should measure 3 inches (7.5 cm) long. Glue one loop to each side of the pine-cone-and-package pick. Tuck the ends of the loops under the pick.

CHRISTMAS REINDEER

Because the colors used in this design blend well with office decor, this would make a novel holiday gift container for a fun-loving businessperson. Filled with Christmas candies, it could also make an interesting conversation piece for a busy company's reception area. See color photograph on page 89.

Intermediate
2 hours
$32 – $36

You will need:

☐ One unfinished wooden reindeer container, 18 inches (45.5 cm) long × 19 inches (48 cm) tall

☐ Copper spray paint

☐ Gold spray paint

- ☐ 2 yards (1.8 m) 1/4-inch-wide (.6 cm) copper metallic braid
- ☐ Three burgundy lotus pods
- ☐ Ten 6-inch (15 cm) preserved pine pieces
- ☐ 6 yards (5.4 m) 7/8-inch-wide (2 cm) red/gold/green patterned Christmas ribbon
- ☐ Six 10-inch (25.5 cm) peacock sword feathers
- ☐ Two 1/2-inch (1.3 cm) movable eyes
- ☐ Glue
- ☐ 30-gauge cloth-covered wire
- ☐ Green floral tape

1. Spray the reindeer container with copper paint.
2. Outline the shape of the front of the reindeer with the copper braid and glue it in place.
3. Make a six-loop bow with 2/3 yard (.6 m) of the ribbon as directed on page 16. Each loop should measure 1 1/2 inches (4 cm). Set aside.
4. Make a ten-loop bow with 2 yards (1.8 m) of ribbon. Each loop should measure 3 inches (7.5 cm) long. Make another ten-loop bow with 2 more yards of ribbon.
5. With the reindeer facing left, glue the smallest bow to the lower portion of the reindeer's right leg.
6. Glue one of the ten-loop bows to the lower left side of the reindeer's body.
7. Glue the last ten-loop bow to the base of the right side of the reindeer's neck.
8. Glue and drape the remaining ribbon from bow to bow starting, at the top of the reindeer's head and working down to the smallest bow.
9. Lightly spray the pods with gold paint. Glue one pod to the center of each bow after removing any stems.
10. Randomly glue various sizes of the preserved pine between the bow loops.
11. Cut the stems of three sword feathers to a length of 1/2 inch (1.3 cm). Bring the end and the tip of the feather together forming an oval shape. Floral tape the end to the tip to keep this shape.
12. Cut the stems of the remaining feathers to 1/2 inch (1.3 cm). Glue the feathers throughout the design as shown above, placing the circular feathers in the center portion of the design and extending the longer feathers to the extremities of the design.

CHRISTMAS BUSHEL FRUIT BASKET

Small Christmas package ornaments dress up this plain red bushel basket. Add fruit to complete the gift. After the fruit is gone, it will make a nice holder for Christmas cards or candy. See color photograph on page 89.

Beginner
30 minutes
$14 – $16

You will need:

- ☐ One round bushel basket, 9 inches (22.5 cm) diameter × 7 inches (17.5 cm) tall
- ☐ Ten 3-inch (7.5 cm) glittered plastic pine sprigs
- ☐ 2 yards (1.8 m) 1¹/₂-inch-wide (4 cm) plaid ribbon
- ☐ One 4-inch (10 cm) flocked novelty Santa
- ☐ Sixteen assorted Christmas package ornaments, 1¹/₂ inches wide (4 cm)
- ☐ Glue
- ☐ 30-gauge cloth-covered wire

1. Make an eight-loop bow with the 1¹/₂-inch (4 cm) ribbon as directed on page 16. Each loop should measure 3 inches (7.5 cm), with two 12-inch (30.5 cm) streamers and no center loop.

2. Glue the bow to the top edge of the basket. Drape and glue the bows streamers about 2 inches (5 cm) from the bottom of the basket.

3. Glue the ten 3-inch (7.5 cm) glittered pine sprigs around the top edge of the bushel basket. Slightly overlap the pine sprigs.

4. Randomly glue the sixteen Christmas packages all the way around the top edge of the basket.

5. Glue the Santa to the basket edge at the right side of the bow.

CHRISTMAS HEART VINE BASKET

This basket will make a lovely addition to anyone's country home decor. The bright red shiny berries, green ivy leaves, and baby's breath create an interesting combination of textures. See color photograph on page 89.

Beginner
I hour
$17 – $19

You will need:

☐ One vine heart basket, 9 inches (22.5 cm) diameter × 8 inches (20 cm) tall × 4 inches (10 cm) deep

☐ 2 ounces preserved baby's breath

☐ Forty 3/8-inch (.9 cm) shiny red holly berries

☐ Fourteen 1 1/2-inch (4 cm) silk ivy leaves

☐ 1 yard (.9 m) 1/4-inch-wide (.6 m) red cotton minidot ribbon

☐ 1 1/2 yards (1.3 m) 3/8-inch-wide (.9 cm) red cotton minidot ribbon

☐ Glue

☐ 30-gauge cloth-covered wire

1. Make a ten-loop bow with 1 1/2 yards (1.3 m) of the 3/8-inch (.9 cm) minidot ribbon as directed on page 16. Each loop should measure 1 1/2 inches (4 cm) with two 3-inch (7.5 cm) streamers. Set aside.

2. Glue one end of the ¹/₄-inch (.6 cm) red cotton minidot ribbon to the base of one side of the handle. Loosely drape and wrap the ribbon around the basket handle. Glue to secure it at the opposite side of the basket handle.

3. Break off small clusters of baby's breath, approximately 1¹/₂ inches (4 cm) long. Glue several clusters at a time to the top edge of the basket.

4. Continue gluing clusters all around the top edge of the basket, overlapping the clusters. Leave no empty spaces.

5. If the berries have wire stems, leave only 1 inch (2.5 cm) of wire attached to the berries. Randomly glue the berries in clusters of three, equally spaced around the edge of the basket. Make sure the wire stems are glued into the baby's breath.

6. Cut the ivy leaves from the main stem of the foliage with scissors or wire cutters. Randomly glue these between the clusters of red berries and baby's breath.

7. Glue the bow to the upper point of the heart basket at the base of the basket handle.

Back: Romantic Victorian Basket.
Front: Wedding Card Basket (left), Lace
and Ribbon Rose Basket (right).

Back: Bridal Gift Bag Grouping (left),
Victorian Box (right). Front: Love Bag
Grouping.

Clockwise from top: Over the Hill Basket, Duffer's Gift Bag, Anniversary Basket, Abaca Heart Basket with Lid, Two-Tiered Easter Basket (with Mylar balloon), Springtime Easter Basket, Valentine Box with Teddy Bear, St. Patrick's Day Shamrock Bag; It's a Boy Gift Bag.

Back: Christmas Basket, Reindeer Basket. Middle: Christmas Heart Vine Basket, Gift from Santa Basket, Christmas Candy Box. Front: Christmas Bushel Basket, Happy Holiday Gift Basket.

Clockwise from top: Spring Gift Basket, Stars and Stripes, Bon Voyage Basket.

Back: Silk Vegetable Basket, Thank You Hostess Basket. Front: Bird's Nest Basket, Basket with Asparagus Fern.

Clockwise from left: Happy Birthday Bear Basket, Mylar Party Bag with favors, Happy Birthday Basket, Mylar Heart Bag.

Clockwise from top: Wine Bag with Feathers and Drieds, Ivy and Daisy Basket, Wine Bag, Corporate Food Basket, Fall Gift Basket, Pasta Primavera Basket.

Back: Porcelain Rose Basket, Umbrella Shower Basket, Ribbon Soap Basket, Peach and Aqua Basket. Front (clockwise from top): Bedroom Boxes, Boudoir Basket, Blue Guest Towel Basket, Ribbon Woven Basket, Little Girl Gift Basket, Seashell Treasure Chest, Baby's Breath Basket.

Back:
Sticker-Decorated
Bags, Sponge
Painting,
Handpainting on a
Lunch Bag, Crayon
Basket. Front:
Sticker-Decorated
Bags, Angel Bag,
Clown Box.

Mother's Day Sewing
Basket, It's a Girl
Gift Basket, Abaca
Heart Box.

Back: Scents and Starters Bag, Necktie Bag, Halloween Bag. Middle: Hearth Basket, Spooky Halloween Treat Basket. Front: Mail Basket, Freeze-Dried Rose Basket.

Wine and Food Designs

*G*ifts for a new home or to thank a hostess usually include wine and some sort of food selections. You'll find many imaginative ideas for wine and food designs in this chapter—from simple decorations involving a paper bag to elaborate baskets filled to the brim with wonderful things to eat and drink.

CORPORATE FOOD BASKET

Advanced
2 hours
$13 – $17

The colors and dried materials used to decorate this gift basket give it a contemporary, corporate look and feel. It would also be a stunning way to present your hostess with some gourmet delights on Thanksgiving or any time during the year. See color photograph on page 91.

You will need:

- [ ] One round whitewashed basket, 11 inches (28 cm) diameter × 20 inches (50.5 cm) tall × 9 inches (22.5 cm) deep
- [ ] 3¹/₂ yards (3.2 m) 3-inch-wide (7.5 cm) metallic floral ribbon
- [ ] One block dry floral foam, 2 inches (5 cm) × 3 inches (7.5 cm) × 2 inches (5 cm)
- [ ] Small amount Spanish moss
- [ ] Three black, curly rattan pieces, 7 inches (17.5 cm), 9 inches (22.5 cm), 10 inches (25.5 cm)
- [ ] Sixteen lengths black, glittered ting ting, lengths from 6 inches (15 cm) to 18 inches (45.5 cm)
- [ ] Four stems metallic gold leaves, lengths from 4 inches (10 cm) to 10 inches (25.5 cm)
- [ ] Five stems red dried branches, lengths from 6 inches (15 cm) to 9 inches (22.5 cm)
- [ ] Glue
- [ ] 30-gauge cloth-covered wire
- [ ] U-shaped pins

1. Form an eight-loop bow with 4-inch (10 cm) loops and two 9-inch (22.5 cm) streamers as directed on page 16. Set aside.
2. Cut a length of ribbon 24 inches long (60.5 cm). Glue the center of the ribbon 1 inch (2.5 cm) from the bottom of the basket. Bring the ends around and glue them together just under the rim of the basket on the other side.
3. Glue the floral foam on top of where the two ends of the ribbon meet. Hold until secure. To add extra strength, use U-shaped pins inserted into the foam from inside the basket out through to the foam.
4. Cover the foam with Spanish moss. Insert pins through the moss and into the foam to secure.
5. Pin and glue the bow to the center of the foam block.
6. Add dried materials in a random manner behind the bow. Dip the stem of each into glue before positioning in the floral foam. Add as many or as few as you would like. The more materials you add, the heavier the design will appear; the less you add, the lighter it will appear.

PASTA PRIMAVERA BASKET

This brightly decorated basket will make a beautiful accent piece to be used after the gift items are gone. It would be very striking used in a European-style kitchen area. Make use of natural materials such as cloves of garlic and dried red peppers to add an extra decorative touch to the basket. See color photograph on page 91.

Intermediate
3 hours
$25 – $30

You will need:

☐ One willow basket, 12 inches (30.5 cm) × 18 inches (45.5 cm) diameter × 14 inches (35 cm) tall × 7 inches deep (17.5 cm)

☐ Hunter green spray paint

☐ Whitewash spray

☐ 2 yards (1.8 m) 2½-inch-wide (6.5 cm) grape motif ribbon

☐ 3 yards (2.7 m) ⅛-inch-wide (.3 cm) red wired satin tubing

☐ 3 yards (2.7 m) ⅛-inch-wide (.3 cm) white wired satin tubing

☐ 3 yards (2.7 m) ⅛-inch-wide (.3 cm) green wired satin tubing

☐ One burlap bag with wooden heart decorative trim, 5 inches (12.5 cm) × 6 inches (15 cm)

☐ Twenty clusters of ⅜-inch (.9 cm) red berries with six berries per cluster

☐ One stem of green onion grass, 12 inches long (30.5 cm)

97

☐ Four 5-inch (12.5 cm) wooden kitchen utensils: rolling pin, mallet, spoon, fork

☐ Three 8-inch (20 cm) dried chili peppers

☐ Five 3-inch (7.5 cm) garlic cloves

☐ Eighteen 2-inch (5 cm) grape leaves

☐ Eighteen 3-inch (7.5 cm) grape leaves

☐ Three 8-inch (20 cm) lasagna noodles

☐ Glue

☐ 30-gauge cloth-covered wire

1. Lightly spray the basket with hunter green spray color. Allow to dry.

2. Spray the whitewash over the hunter green. While the whitewash is still wet, gently wipe some of it away to allow some of the green color to show through. Allow to dry.

3. Braid together the 3-yard (2.7 m) lengths of the three colors of wired satin tubing following directions on page 15.

4. Starting at a point 7 inches (17.5 cm) from one end of the grape ribbon, glue to the base of one side of the basket handle.

5. Gather and tie the ribbon at 4-inch (10 cm) intervals with 2-inch (5 cm) lengths of cloth-covered wire. Glue the ribbon to the top edge of the basket at the points where the ribbon is gathered with wire. Overlap the ends of the ribbon at the base of the basket handle.

6. Cut the stems of the eighteen 2-inch (5 cm) and eighteen 3-inch (7.5 cm) grape leaves to a length of 1 inch (2.5 cm). Glue one leaf at each point where the ribbon is gathered and glued to the edge of the basket.

7. Randomly glue the rest of the leaves around the edge of the basket and on the basket handle.

8. Make a four-loop bow at each end of the braided satin tubing as directed on page 16. The loops should measure 3 inches (7.5 cm) long with no center loop.

9. Glue one bow to one side of the basket at the base of the handle.

10. Very loosely wrap and drape the braided tubing around the basket handle.

11. Glue the other braided bow to the opposite side of the basket handle.

12. Cut the stems of the berry clusters to a length of 1 inch (2.5 cm). Glue one berry cluster to the center of each braided bow.

13. Glue one berry cluster to the top edge of the basket at each point where the grape leaf ribbon has been gathered and glued.

14. Glue the rest of the berry clusters around the basket handle.

15. With cloth-covered wire, attach the burlap bag to one side of the base of the basket handle. Allow the bag to drape over the side of the basket. Fill the bag with lasagna noodles.

16. Glue the chili peppers to the side of the basket handle just above the burlap bag. Be sure they are positioned at different heights going up the side of the handle.

17. Separate the onion grass into five bunches of four leaves each. With scissors, carefully curl the ends of the onion grass bunches (use the same process you would use to curl ribbon). Glue each bunch to the handle and basket edge between the chili peppers and to each side of the burlap bag.

18. Glue two wooden kitchen utensils behind the braided bow at the base of each side of the basket handle.

19. Tie various lengths of cloth-covered wire around five cloves of garlic. Secure to the top center of the basket handle with the wire. Allow the garlic cloves to drape down below the basket handle.

WINE BAG

A bunch of grapes and coordinating ribbon make even this plain brown bag look very attractive. See color photo page 91.

Beginner
20 minutes
$9 – $11

You will need:

☐ One brown paper wine bottle bag, 4 inches (10 cm) × 15 inches (38 cm)

☐ Purple webbing spray paint

☐ Copper webbing spray paint

☐ 1¹/₂ yards (1.3 m) 2¹/₂-inch-wide (6.5 cm) white grape-patterned ribbon

☐ One bunch of plastic grapes, 8 inches (20 cm)

☐ 30-gauge cloth-covered wire

1. Spray the bag with the purple and copper webbing paint. Allow to dry.

2. Make a six-loop bow as directed on page 16. The loops should measure 3¹/₂ inches long (8.8 cm) with two 4-inch (10 cm) streamers. Secure the bow with an 18-inch-long (45.5 cm) piece of cloth-covered wire.

3. Using the wire from the bow, attach the bow to the bunch of grapes.

4. Place the bottle of wine in the bag.

5. Gather the top of the bag. Secure the bag closed with the wire attached to the bow and grapes. Allow the grapes to drape down the front of the bag.

WINE BAG WITH FEATHERS AND DRIEDS

This design contains some unusual decorative floral items. Rolled paper roses, elegant metallic ribbon, and peacock and pheasant feathers combine to make a stunning and high-style impact. The design is created on a removable floral foam base that could be removed and attached to a wreath or used as a small decorative table accent. See color photo on page 91.

You will need:

☐ One paisley-print wine bag with handles, 6 inches (15 cm) × 13 inches (32.5 cm)

☐ One Mini Deco foam holder

☐ 3 yards (2.7 m) 1¹/₂-inch-wide (4 cm) copper/gold metallic ribbon

☐ Five peacock feathers

☐ Five 1-inch (2.5 cm) ivory rolled parchment roses

☐ Five pheasant feathers

☐ 1-ounce bunch dried peach statice

☐ Two curved dried strelitzia, one 9 inches (22.5 cm), one 13 inches (32.5 cm)

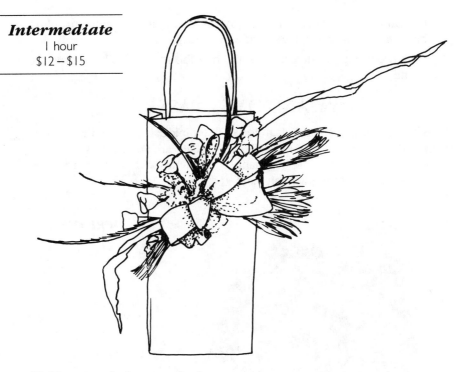

Intermediate
I hour
$12 – $15

☐ 30-gauge cloth-covered wire

☐ Glue

☐ U-shaped pins

1. Cut the ribbon into two 1¹/2-yard (1.3 m) lengths. With one piece, make an eight-loop bow, as described on page 16, with 3-inch (7.5 cm) loops. Make a second bow with the second piece of ribbon.

2. Attach the two bows to the foam holder with U-shaped pins. Make sure the loops evenly cover all the sides of the holder.

3. Dip the stem of the longer strelitzia branch into glue. Position the branch into the top section of the foam holder.

4. Position the shorter strelitzia branch into the bottom of the foam holder. The curves of the branches should form an S shape.

5. Cut the stems of five parchment roses to lengths of 4 inches (10 cm). Dip each stem into glue before positioning it into the foam. Position the roses in an arch pattern along the left side of the design placing them in between the ribbon loops.

6. Cut five peacock feathers to a length of 6 inches (15 cm). Dip them in glue and place them to the right side of the design in an arch pattern.

7. Cut five pheasant feathers to a length of 6 inches (15 cm). Dip them in glue and place them into the floral foam between the roses.

8. Cut bunches of statice 2 inches (5 cm) long. Dip into glue and fill in between the bow loops to cover any empty spots.

9. Glue the holder to the center of the bag about 4 inches below the top of the bag.

IVY AND DAISY BASKET

This basket has a crisp and clean look. The pink daisies are a bright contrast to the dark green ivy leaves. The ivy leaves are an easy base to work with, and the flowers can be changed to blend with any occasion or decor. See color photograph on page 91.

Beginner
I hour
$14–$17

You will need:

☐ One heavy willow basket, 9 inches (22.5 cm) diameter × 12 inches (30.5 cm) tall

☐ Forty-eight 1¾-inch (4.3 cm) × 2-inch (5 cm) silk ivy leaves*

☐ Thirteen 1¾-inch (4.3 cm) pink silk daisies

☐ Nineteen 1-inch (2.5 cm) pink silk gypsophila flowers

☐ Glue

*You may need more or less ivy leaves and flowers depending on the size of your basket.

1. Cut all ivy leaves from the main stem of the ivy spray.

2. Use thirty-two leaves to cover the top edge of the basket. Starting at the basket handle, glue eight leaves to the top basket edge, angling them away from the handle. Repeat this step three more times, starting at the basket handle. When you are through, the edge of the basket should be completely covered.

3. The handle is covered by sixteen leaves. Start at the middle of the handle and glue eight leaves angling them down one side of the basket handle. Repeat with the last eight leaves to the opposite side of the handle.

4. Glue the daisies in a random manner around the basket edge and handle. Be sure to evenly distribute the flowers within the design.

5. Glue the tiny gypsophila flowers randomly throughout the design filling in any empty spaces.

FALL GIFT BASKET

The design of this basket is concentrated on the handle. It would make a lovely hostess gift for a Thanksgiving dinner party. The basket could be filled with your hostess' favorite tea or coffee. Include gourmet cookies or biscuits to share with her guests. See color photograph on page 91.

Beginner
I hour
$12–$15

You will need:

☐ One oval basket, 9 inches (22.5 cm) × 12 inches (30.5 cm) diameter × 11 inches (28 cm) tall × 2 inches (5 cm) deep

☐ Eight 3-inch (7.5 cm) silk fall leaves

- [ ] Nine ⁵/₈-inch (1.5 cm) orange fall berry clusters
- [ ] 2 ounces German statice
- [ ] Glue

1. Cut the stems of the berry clusters to a length of 1 inch (2.5 cm).
2. Glue the stems of each cluster to the handle of the basket. Equally space the clusters to cover the whole basket handle.
3. Glue the eight fall leaves in between the berry clusters to the basket handle.
4. Finish by gluing 2-inch (5 cm) bunches of German statice to the basket handle, filling in any empty spaces between the berry clusters and leaves.

SILK VEGETABLE BASKET

This unusual style basket lends itself well to the rich design created with the silk vegetables. It would be a beautiful addition to a very large country kitchen. See color photograph on page 90.

Beginner
45 minutes
$18 – $22

You will need:

- [ ] One flat cane basket, 12 inches (30.5 cm) diameter × 16 inches (40.5 cm) tall × 2¹/₂ inches (6.5 cm) deep
- [ ] 4 yards (3.6 m) 1¹/₂-inch-wide (4 cm) pale green webbed ribbon

- ☐ 4 yards (3.6 m) 1¹/2-inch-wide (4 cm) peach webbed ribbon
- ☐ Four 8-inch (20 cm) silk asparagus
- ☐ One 3¹/2-inch (8.8 cm) silk tomato
- ☐ One 7-inch (17.5 cm) silk leaf lettuce
- ☐ Two 5-inch (12.5 cm) silk green peppers
- ☐ One 8-inch (20 cm) silk cucumber
- ☐ One 5-inch (12.5 cm) silk red cabbage
- ☐ One 6-inch (15 cm) silk endive
- ☐ One 4-inch (10 cm) silk onion
- ☐ One 12-inch (30.5 cm) silk celery stalk
- ☐ Three 2¹/2-inch (6.5 cm) silk mushrooms
- ☐ Two 3-inch (7.5 cm) silk mushrooms
- ☐ Three 4-inch (10 cm) silk radishes with leaves
- ☐ Glue
- ☐ 30-gauge cloth-covered wire

1. All the vegetables are clustered at one side of the basket handle. Glue the leaf lettuce to the basket edge horizontally at the right side of the basket handle.
2. Glue the red cabbage to the basket edge at the left side of the handle.
3. Glue the celery stalk in a vertical position to the basket handle, about 5 inches (12.5 cm) from the base of the basket.
4. Glue two asparagus to each side of the celery stalk at the handle, stacking them in an upwards direction.
5. Glue two green peppers to the basket handle, left of the celery stalk, near the base of the handle.
6. Glue the cucumber to the left of the green peppers in a vertical position.
7. Glue the onion and tomato on each side of the handle into the heart of the design.
8. Randomly glue the mushrooms and two of the radishes to fill in spaces within the design.
9. Cut the green mesh ribbon into two 1¹/2-yard (1.3 m) lengths and one 1-yard (.9 m) length. Cut the peach ribbon the same way.
10. Form a layered bow with 1¹/2 yards (1.3 m) of the peach and green ribbon as directed on page 18. The loops should measure 4 inches (10 cm). Form a second identical bow.
11. Glue one bow to the base of the basket on the same side with the vegetable cluster.

12. Glue the second bow to the base of the basket handle at the side opposite the cluster of vegetables. Glue one radish into the center of this bow.

13. Glue the two ends of the remaining ribbons to the base of the basket handle behind the bow decorating the side with the vegetable cluster.

14. Loosely wrap and drape the remaining ribbon around the basket handle.

15. Secure the ends of the ribbon near the bow at the opposite side of the handle.

Bed and Bath Designs

*D*esigns containing towels and soaps as well as a variety of personal grooming items are popular gifts. Why not have one waiting for a special friend next time they spend the night with you. The designs in this chapter are also useful for decorating the rooms in your own home; or can be used as a housewarming gift.

BLUE GUEST TOWEL BASKET

Beginner
45 minutes
$14–$17

This basket, filled with guest bathroom towels and fancy soaps, would make an elegant housewarming gift. Because of the nature of the iridescent flowers used, this design would be perfect to accent a powder room wallpapered in a foil pattern. See color photograph on page 92.

You will need:

- [ ] One blue rectangular basket, 8¹/₂ inches (21.3 cm) × 9¹/₂ inches (23.8 cm) diameter × 10 inches (25.5 cm) tall × 5 inches (12.5 cm) deep
- [ ] Four multicolor (mauve, aqua, silver tones) lamé roses with leaves 3 inches in diameter (7.5 cm)
- [ ] Three multicolor (mauve, aqua, silver tones) lamé tiger lilies 5 inches in diameter (12.5 cm)
- [ ] Glue

1. Remove all rose heads from the main stem of the flower by gently pulling them off the main stem. Remove the leaves in this same manner. Remove the lily heads in the same manner.
2. Glue one rose to each side of the basket where the handle and basket come together.
3. Glue a lily head to the top center of the basket handle.
4. Glue a rose head on each side of the center lily, about 2 inches (5 cm) away from the lily.
5. Glue a lily on the basket handle above each of the first two roses positioned. The lily should be centered between the two roses in place on either side of it.
6. Complete the design by gluing rose leaves to fill in any open areas.

BEDROOM BOXES

The dark, rich colors of the miniature hat boxes pictured on the next page are enhanced by pearl loops and sheer fabric ribbon. Grouping the three boxes together creates a lovely display. See color photograph on page 92.

You will need:

- [ ] One navy floral-patterned hat box, 7 inches (17.5 cm) diameter × 2³/₄ inches (6.8 cm) deep
- [ ] One navy floral-patterned hat box, 8 inches (20 cm) diameter × 3¹/₄ inches (8.1 cm) deep
- [ ] One navy floral-patterned hat box, 9 inches (22.5 cm) diameter × 4 inches (10 cm) deep
- [ ] Two stems navy open roses with 3-inch (7.5 cm) heads
- [ ] 4 yards (3.6 m) 1¹/₂-inch-wide (4 cm) blue sheer picot-edged ribbon

Beginner
1 1/2 hours
$20 – $25

- ☐ 2 yards (1.8 m) 1/8-inch-wide (.3 cm) blue sparkling ribbon
- ☐ Twelve 2-inch (5 cm) peach circular pearl stems
- ☐ Glue
- ☐ 30-gauge cloth-covered wire

1. Cut two 1-yard (.9 m) lengths of the 1 1/2-inch-wide ribbon. Place the 8-inch (20 cm) box on top of the 9-inch (22.5 cm) box. Wrap the ribbon around both boxes and tie together at the top. Tie again with the second piece of ribbon criss-crossing the first length of ribbon.

2. Cut the remaining 2 yards (1.8 m) of sheer picot ribbon into twelve 6-inch (15 cm) lengths. Cut all the ends of the ribbon at an angle. Set aside.

3. Cut the 2 yards (1.8 m) of 1/8-inch (.3 cm) blue ribbon into twelve 6-inch (15 cm) lengths. Cut all the ribbon ends at an angle.

4. Place six 6-inch (15 cm) lengths of the sheer picot ribbon and six 6-inch (15 cm) lengths of the blue ribbon together. Wrap around the center of the cluster with cloth-covered wire. Pull each length of ribbon apart to fill out the bow and make it fluffy.

5. Repeat step 4 to make a second bow.

6. Glue one bow to the center top of the two hat boxes tied together. Glue the second bow to the top center of the 7-inch (17.5 cm) box.

7. Remove the two rose heads from their wire stems. Glue the rose heads to the center of each of the bows.

8. Cut the stems of the pearl stems to a length of ¹/₂ inch (1.3 cm). Glue six pearl loops in between the ribbon loops of the 7-inch (17.5 cm) box. Do the same with the remaining six pearl loops, attaching them to the bow on top of the double boxes.

9. Remove the rose leaves from the wire stems. Glue the leaves underneath the roses at the center of each bow.

FUSCHIA AND BLACK BOUDOIR BASKET

The colors of this gift basket do not lend itself to decorate within the color scheme of just any room. The colors are sensual and intimate. Fill this gift basket with scented oils, bath beads, or other romantic items. Of course, you could change the colors to coordinate them to any occasion or decor. It would make a fun gift for a personal bridal shower. See color photograph on page 92.

Beginner
I hour
$15 – $20

You will need:

☐ One fireside basket, 14 inches (35 cm) × 10 inches (25.5 cm) diameter × 9 inches (22.5 cm) high
☐ Fuschia spray paint
☐ 2 yards (1.8 m) 2¹/₂-inch-wide (6.5 cm) fuschia/black gathered lace
☐ 2 yards (1.8 m) 6-inch-wide (15 cm) fuschia tulle
☐ 4 yards (3.6 m) ¹/₈-inch-wide (.3 cm) black satin ribbon
☐ 4 yards (3.6 m) ¹/₈-inch-wide (.3 cm) fuschia satin ribbon
☐ 4 yards (3.6 m) 2 mm fused white pearls

☐ Three 6-inch (15 cm) lengths of ivy with seven 1-inch (2.5 cm) leaves per length

☐ Three 3-inch (7.5 cm) fuschia open roses

☐ One stem silk baby's breath with twelve 3-inch (7.5 cm) clusters

☐ Glue

1. Spray the basket with fuschia spray color. Allow to dry.

2. Glue the black/fuschia lace trim to the outside of the basket edge. "Poof" the tulle and glue it in several locations around the edge of the basket.

3. Make a braid using 4 yards (3.6 m) each of the black satin ribbon, fuschia satin ribbon, and fused pearls as directed on page 15.

4. Starting at the base of one of the basket handles, glue the braid to the gathered edge of the lace trim.

5. At the base of the handle where the braid meets, wrap at 1 1/2-inch (4 cm) intervals around the basket handle to the other side of the handle. Trim and glue the braid to secure in place.

6. Glue a T formation of ivy to one side of the basket handle. Do this by gluing one spray up the handle and one spray on the basket edge on each side of the handle.

7. Glue the three roses in a cluster near the base of the basket handle.

8. Cut the silk baby's breath into 3-inch (7.5 cm) lengths.

9. Randomly glue the sprigs of baby's breath between the roses and ivy.

LITTLE GIRL GIFT BASKET

The project shown on the next page would be a darling gift basket for a little girl. It would give her room an extra little feminine touch. See color photograph on page 92.

You will need:

☐ One oval pink/white basket with doll face attached to front, 6 inches (15 cm) × 8 inches (20 cm) diameter, 9 inches (22.5 cm) high × 4 inches (10 cm) deep

☐ Six 1 1/4-inch (3.1 cm) fuschia rosebuds

☐ Six 1 1/4-inch (3.1 cm) light pink rosebuds

☐ 2 1/2 yards (2.3 m) 3/4-inch-wide (1.8 cm) hot pink wired edged ribbon

☐ Forty-eight 3 mm white pearl stems

☐ White floral tape

☐ Glue

☐ 30-gauge cloth-covered wire

Beginner
1 hour
$17 – $22

1. Make an eight-loop bow using the 2¹/₂ yards (2.3 m) of hot pink ribbon as directed on page 16. The loops should measure 3 inches (7.5 cm) long and have two 18-inch (45.5 cm) streamers.
2. Glue this bow to the top center of the basket handle.
3. Floral tape three fuschia rosebuds and three light pink rosebuds into a cluster.
4. Floral tape twenty-four of the white pearl stems into this cluster throughout the roses. Allow the pearl stems to extend 1 inch (2.5 cm) above the rosebuds.
5. Make a second flower cluster in the same manner as described in steps 3 and 4.
6. Cut both of the flower cluster stems to a length of 1 inch (2.5 cm). Be sure the ends are securely floral taped.
7. Glue these two clusters into the top center of the bow, overlapping the stems of the clusters to conceal them.
8. Curl the streamers and drape them down toward the basket.

RIBBON WOVEN BASKET

This type of basket comes in many different sizes. The cut ribbon lengths will need to be adapted to the size of the basket. Each basket will take on a different look because of the types of ribbon you use. See color photograph on page 92.

Beginner
45 minutes
$9 – $12

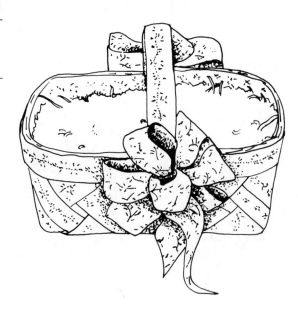

You will need:

☐ One rectangular woven basket, 5 inches (12.5 cm) × 7 inches (17.5 cm) diameter × 6 inches (15 cm) high × 3 inches (7.5 cm) deep

☐ 2 yards (1.8 m) 5/8-inch-wide (1.5 cm) peach/blue floral ribbon

☐ 3 yards (2.7 m) 7/8-inch-wide (2 cm) blue floral ribbon

☐ 1 yard (.9 m) 7/8-inch-wide (2 cm) peach floral ribbon

☐ 1 yard (.9 m) 7/8-inch-wide (2 cm) coordinating ribbon

☐ Glue

☐ 30-gauge cloth-covered wire

1. Make a six-loop bow with 1 yard (.9 m) of the 7/8-inch (2 cm) blue floral ribbon as directed on page 16. Loops should measure 2 inches (5 cm) with two 4-inch (10 cm) streamers.

2. Cover the basket handle by gluing a length of the 5/8-inch (1.5 cm) peach/blue floral ribbon over the top of the handle and a length of the same type of ribbon to the underside. Trim excess ribbon.

3. Weave 1 yard (.9 m) of the blue floral ribbon into the weave of the basket, completely covering that particular section. Trim to fit.

4. Continue weaving the ribbon until all sections of the basket are covered. Alternate the ribbon patterns around the basket.

5. Glue the bow to the base of the basket handle at one side of the basket.

MAUVE BOX WITH DRIED ROSES

This is a perfect box to hold some rose-scented potpourri. Actual dried rosebuds could be glued to the design on the lid of the box. You may use the new dried-look silk roses in place of the real ones. See color photograph on page 89.

Beginner
30 minutes
$12 – $14

You will need:

☐ One round chipboard box, 4¹/₂ inches (11.3 cm) diameter × 2 inches (5 cm) deep

☐ Mauve acrylic paint

☐ Five 1-inch (2.5 cm) burgundy dried-look rosebuds

☐ Six 3-inch (7.5 cm) sprigs ivory lily of the valley

☐ ²/₃ yards (.6 m) ¹/₂-inch-wide (1.3 cm) pink lace-edged ribbon

☐ ¹/₂ yard (.5 m) 1¹/₄-inch-wide (3.1 cm) pink lace-edged ribbon

☐ Eight 2-inch (5 cm) sprigs preserved maiden-hair fern

☐ Glue

☐ Paintbrush

☐ 30-gauge cloth-covered wire

1. Paint the box mauve (or your choice of color). Allow to dry.

2. Glue the 1¹/₄-inch-wide (3.1 cm) ribbon around the bottom edge of the box.

3. Cut the 1/2-inch (1.3 cm) ribbon into eight 3-inch (7.5 cm) lengths. Make single loops as described on page 13.

4. Glue the lily-of-the-valley sprigs in a crescent pattern to the left side of the lid of the box. Angle three sprigs upward and three downward. Follow the curved line of the lid for placement of the flowers. The design should cover only half of the lid of the box.

5. Remove the stems of five dried-look rosebuds and glue into the design, angling three up and two down.

6. Glue the ribbon loops randomly between the lily of the valley and the rosebuds, filling in empty spaces.

7. Randomly glue the eight sprigs of maiden-hair fern into the design.

PORCELAIN ROSE BASKET

The porcelain roses in this arrangement are a perfect complement to the design on the front of this basket. You can buy the porcelain roses or make your own. Fill the basket with potpourri, and you have a lovely addition to any bedroom or bath. See color photograph on page 92.

Intermediate
1 1/2 hours
$20 – $24

You will need:

☐ One rectangular white basket with three-dimensional pink rose decorations, 9 inches (22.5 cm) × 12 inches (30.5 cm) diameter × 14 inches (35 cm) tall × 6 inches (15 cm) deep

☐ One block dry floral foam, 3 inches (7.5 cm) × 3 inches (7.5 cm)

☐ Three 2-inch (5 cm) white porcelain roses

☐ Three 2-inch (5 cm) medium pink porcelain roses

☐ Two 2-inch (5 cm) deep pink porcelain roses

☐ Nine 8-inch (20 cm) Boston fern leaves

☐ Spanish moss to cover foam

☐ Potpourri to fill basket

☐ U-shaped craft pins

☐ Glue

1. Glue the block of foam into the bottom of the basket, positioning it on the left side. Cover the foam with moss and insert craft pins through the moss and into the foam to secure.

2. Cut the stems of the roses as follows:

    white roses:
        one 6-inch (15 cm) length
        one 7-inch (17.5 cm) length
        one 11-inch (28 cm) length
    medium pink roses:
        one 6-inch (15 cm) length
        one 9-inch (22.5 cm) length
        one 15-inch (38 cm) length
    deep pink roses:
        one 7-inch (17.5 cm) length
        one 11-inch (28 cm) length

3. Position the tallest flowers into the floral foam toward the back of the arrangement. Position the shortest flowers into the floral foam to the front of the basket.

4. Randomly position the Boston fern leaves into the arrangement, filling in the spaces between the roses. Gently shape the leaves to give them a more natural appearance.

5. Fill the basket with potpourri. Allow the potpourri to cover the floral foam.

RIBBON SOAP BASKET

This pretty floral ribbon, box-pleated around a basket, makes a cheerful accent to any bath decor. Fill with pretty soaps or bath items. See color photograph on page 92.

Beginner
1 hour
$10 – $13

You will need:

☐ One oval cane basket, 8 inches (20 cm) × 6 inches (15 cm) diameter × 3¹/₂ inches (8.8 cm) deep

☐ 4 yards 2³/₄-inch-wide (6.8 cm) pink floral ribbon

☐ 1¹/₃ (1.2 m) yards ¹/₄-inch-wide (.6 cm) pink fused pearls

☐ Glue

☐ Stapler

1. Make 1-inch (2.5 cm) box pleats on one edge of the ribbon as shown.

2. Glue the pleated ribbon around the edge of the basket just below the rim. You will be gluing the pleated edge to the basket.

3. Cut a 24-inch (60.5 cm) length of ribbon. Glue it to the top edge of the box pleats, overlapping slightly to cover the staples. Fold the rest of the ribbon over the edge of the basket and glue around the inside of the basket, pleating the ribbon as needed for a smooth finish.

4. Cut a 20-inch (50.5 cm) length of ribbon. Glue this to the inside of the basket.

5. Cut two 6-inch (15 cm) pieces of ribbon. Round the corners of one side of each piece of ribbon, and glue it to cover the bottom of the basket. Allow the straight edges to overlap slightly.

6. Cut the fused pearls into two 24-inch (60.5 cm) lengths. Glue both lengths around the top edge of the basket to form a double row of pearls. The pearls will cover the glued-edge seam of the ribbon.

To Fill Basket:

You will need:

☐ Decorative soaps
☐ Clear cellophane
☐ 1/2-yard (.5 m) length 2 mm fused pearls
☐ Rubber band

1. Cut a large square of cellophane and place the soaps in the center. Bring all the ends up to one location and secure with rubber band.

2. Tie a bow around the rubber band using the fused pearls.

BABY'S BREATH BASKET

Fill the center of this basket with fragrant potpourri to elegantly scent your bedroom or bath. Decorate the handles and rims of any basket that will fit with the decor of these rooms. See color photograph on page 92.

You will need:

☐ One oval, flat, open basket; 9 inches (22.5 cm) × 10 inches (25.5 cm) diameter × 12 inches (30.5 cm) tall
☐ 4-ounce bunch bleached glittered baby's breath
☐ 3 yards (2.7 m) 1/2-inch-wide (1.3 cm) mauve woven-edge ribbon
☐ 2-ounce bunch purple statice
☐ 3-ounce bunch pink campo flowers
☐ Seven dried-look burgundy rosebuds
☐ 2-ounce bunch rose-colored caspia
☐ 2 yards (1.8 m) 2 mm fused pearls
☐ Six 18-inch lengths of cloth-covered wire
☐ White floral tape
☐ Glue
☐ Potpourri of your choice to fill basket.

1. Holding two pieces of cloth-covered wire together, floral-tape two other pieces end to end, with the first two overlapping 4 inches (10 cm). Measure wire around the top of the handle and cut to fit.

2. Form small 2-inch (5 cm) to 3-inch (7.5 cm) bunches of baby's breath and floral tape these sections to the wire. Place a second bunch of baby's breath below the first, and tape it in place. Continue to floral tape clusters of baby's breath until the wire is covered.

3. Break off 2-inch (5 cm) pieces of baby's breath and glue around the basket rim.

4. Pinch the ribbon and secure it with a 1-inch (2.5 cm) length of cloth-covered wire every 6 inches (15 cm). Glue the pinched portion into the baby's breath circling the rim and handle.

5. Break off statice heads and glue throughout the baby's breath. Make small bunches of six to eight campo flowers, and glue them around the baby's breath. Make small bunches of rose-colored caspia and glue throughout the baby's breath.

6. Equally space the seven rosebuds throughout the baby's breath.

7. Drape and loop the purple pearls around the rim of the basket and handle. Secure with glue at several points throughout the design.

ABACA HEART BOX
WITH SATIN ROSES AND PEARLS

This basket is a quick, easy, and elegant gift item. Fill with potpourri, fancy soaps, etc. See color photograph on page 93.

Intermediate
2 hours
$26 – $32

You will need:

☐ One abaca heart box with lid, 6 inches (15 cm) × 3 inches (7.5 cm) deep

☐ One stem mauve satin roses with three 2-inch (5 cm) open roses and three 1-inch (2.5 cm) buds

☐ Seven 2-inch white circular pearl stems

☐ 2 yards (1.8 m) $^5/_8$-inch-wide (1.5 cm) pink satin lace-edged ribbon

☐ Glue

☐ 30-gauge cloth-covered wire

1. Glue the ribbon around the bottom edge of the basket and around the outside edge of the lid.

2. Cut the remaining ribbon six 5-inch (12.5 cm) lengths. Make six single ribbon loops as directed on page 13.

3. Glue loops to the center of the lid forming a star pattern. Equally space the loops. The edge of the loops should be even with the edge of the basket.

4. Glue the three open roses to the center of the basket lid, covering the wired ends of the ribbon loops.

5. Glue the three buds around the large rose cluster, equally spacing them around the center.

6. Randomly glue the leaves and pearl loops in between the roses and buds to fill in the design.

SEASHELL TREASURE CHEST

This basket is quickly and easily created using glue, assorted seashells, and a fishnet-like ribbon. It would make an excellent container for a gentleman's gift items, or you could fill it with powder-room necessities for a clever housewarming gift. See color photograph on page 92.

Beginner
45 minutes
$10 – $12

You will need:

☐ One wicker box with lid attached, 4¹/₂ inches (11.3 cm) × 8 inches (20 cm)

☐ 1 yard (.9 m) 1³/₄-inch-wide (4.3 cm) mesh ribbon

☐ Approximately 20 assorted seashells, ¹/₂ inch (1.3 cm) to 2 inches (5 cm) in length

☐ Glue

☐ 30-gauge cloth-covered wire

1. Cut the mesh ribbon to fit around the base of the basket. Attach with glue starting at the back of the basket.

2. Gather the mesh ribbon with a small piece of cloth-covered wire at the center front of the basket. Glue this gathered spot to the basket. Continue attaching the mesh ribbon around the other sides and ending at the back.

3. In a random manner, glue ten seashells to the front of the basket on top of the mesh ribbon.

4. Glue a cluster of ten seashells to the top center of the basket lid.

5. Using 6 inches (15 cm) of the mesh ribbon, form a ribbon loop as directed on page 13. Secure with cloth-covered wire. Form a second loop in the same manner.

6. Attach each ribbon loop with glue to the top of the basket lid, tucking the ends of the ribbon loops into the glued cluster of seashells.

CHAPTER 8

All Through the House

A variety of decorated baskets and bags are perfect home-decorating accents. Look through the designs in this chapter to get your creative juices started. Some of the designs are perfect for housewarming gifts, as well.

FREEZE-DRIED ROSE BASKET

Beginner
45 minutes
$13 – $15

This basket has a very soft Victorian look. The roses are actually freeze dried and, therefore, retain much of their color intensity. Statice and sheer ribbon are added as key elements. See color photograph on page 94.

You will need:

☐ One rectangular white basket, 6 inches (15 cm) × 8 inches (20 cm) diameter × 10 inches (25.5 cm) tall × 4 inches (10 cm) deep

☐ Five 1¹/₂-inch (4 cm) freeze-dried roses (These are available from most local florist shops. If you are unable to find them, substitute dried roses.)

☐ 2-ounce bunch German statice

☐ 2¹/₂ yards (2.3 m) 1¹/₂-inch-wide (4 cm) sheer pink woven-edge ribbon

☐ Glue

☐ 30-gauge cloth-covered wire

1. Cut a 1-yard (.9 m) length of ribbon. Make a six-loop bow as directed on page 16. Loops should measure 2¹/₂ inches (6.5 cm) with no center loop and two 3-inch (7.5 cm) streamers.

2. Glue the bow to one side of the base of the basket handle.

3. Cut two 12-inch (30.5 cm) lengths of the sheer pink ribbon. Make a 3-inch (7.5 cm) ribbon loop with a 6-inch (15 cm) streamer as directed on page 13. Repeat to form a second loop.

4. Glue the bow loops vertically along the edge of the basket, one on either side of the bow. The streamers should angle away from the bow.

5. With the remaining length of ribbon, make two loops. Glue these going up the handle. The loop should be angled up and away from the bow.

6. Glue one of the dried roses to the center of the bow. The other four roses should be equally spaced up the handle and to each side of the bow.

7. Break off 3-inch (7.5 cm) pieces of the statice. Glue between the roses and ribbon loops.

MAIL BASKET

This mail basket (see photo next page) would make a lovely housewarming gift filled with pretty stationery or kitchen items. The colors could be changed easily to coordinate with any decor. See color photograph on page 94.

Beginner
1 hour
$12 – $15

You will need:

☐ One flat wall basket with handle, 14 inches (35 cm) tall × 11 inches (28 cm) long × 5 inches (12.5 cm) × 4¹/₂ inches (11.3 cm) deep

☐ 4¹/₂ yards (4.1 m) 1³/₈-inch-wide (3.6 cm) green/mauve fabric ribbon

☐ 3 yards (7.5 cm) 1³/₈-inch-wide (3.6 cm) mauve lace-edged ribbon

☐ Glue

☐ 30-gauge cloth-covered wire

1. Weave the green/mauve ribbon and the mauve lace-edged ribbon into the slats of the basket. Cut and glue alternating ribbons to completely cover the basket.

2. Glue the remaining mauve lace-edged ribbon on the top of the basket handle and all around the basket edge.

3. Cut two 18-inch (45.5 cm) lengths of the green/mauve ribbon. Make two small two-loop bows as directed on page 13. Glue one bow to each side of the base of the basket handle.

4. Make a six-loop bow with the remaining green/mauve ribbon. Loops should measure 2¹/₂ inches (6.5 cm) with two 3-inch (7.5 cm) streamers. Glue the bow to the top center of the basket handle.

BIRD'S NEST BASKET

Dried flowers, pretty floral ribbon, and a feathered bird create an eye-catching arrangement on one side of this basket. See color photograph on page 90.

Beginner
I hour
$12—$15

You will need:

- ☐ One round wicker basket, 10 inches (25.5 cm) diameter × 10 inches (25.5 cm) tall × 3¹/₂ inches (8.8 cm) deep
- ☐ 1 yard 1³/₈-inch-wide (3.4 cm) blue floral fabric ribbon
- ☐ Blue spray paint
- ☐ One 3-inch (7.5 cm) bird's nest
- ☐ Six 1-inch (2.5 cm) robin eggs
- ☐ 1 ounce sphagnum moss
- ☐ One 4-inch (10 cm) deep-blue feathered bird
- ☐ 2-ounce package German statice
- ☐ 2-ounce package pink campo flowers
- ☐ 2-ounce package ivory campo flowers
- ☐ 2-ounce package peach gypsy grass
- ☐ Glue
- ☐ 30-gauge cloth-covered wire

1. Spray basket with blue spray. Allow to dry.

2. Glue a 5-inch (12.5 cm) section of moss to the center of the side of the basket near the base of the handle.

3. Make a four-loop tailored bow with 1 yard (.9 m) of ribbon, following the instructions on page 20. Glue the bow to the moss at the base of the handle.

4. Glue six eggs into the bird's nest. Glue the bird's nest to the top edge of the basket next to the bow. Glue the bird to the top of the bird's nest.

5. Break off 3-inch (7.5 cm) pieces of statice. Glue these to the top edge of the basket to cover an area of about 10 inches (25.5 cm).

6. Break off 2-inch (5 cm) pieces of the peach gypsy grass and the pink and ivory campo flowers. Glue randomly into the statice, around the nest and bow.

SCENTS AND STARTERS BAG

Beginner
I hour
$16 – $20

Fill this bag with potpourri or gift items to be used in a family room, such as long fireplace matches, starter logs, and so on. It would give any family room a warm feeling. See color photograph on page 94.

You will need:

☐ One printed canvas bag, 9 inches (22.5 cm) × 20 inches (50.5 cm)

☐ Four 18-inch (45.5 cm) long cinnamon sticks

☐ 1 yard (.9 m) 4-inch-wide (10 cm) peach paper ribbon

☐ 1 yard (.9 m) 2-inch-wide (5 cm) green/peach floral ribbon

☐ 3 yards (2.7 m) untwisted paper ribbon

☐ One 1¹/₂-inch (4 cm) glass potpourri ball with cork

☐ 2 ounces potpourri of your choice

☐ 30-gauge cloth-covered wire

☐ Chenille stem

1. Tie the four cinnamon sticks together with the untwisted ribbon. Secure at one end of the 3-yard (2.7 m) length. Set aside.

2. Holding the 1-yard (.9 m) length of floral ribbon on top of the 1-yard (.9 m) length of peach paper ribbon, make a four-loop bow as directed on page 16. Loops should measure 4 inches (10 cm) with no center loop and with two 8-inch (20 cm) streamers. Set aside.

3. Fill the bag with gift items. Gather the bag together and secure it with the chenille stem.

4. Tie the bow to the cinnamon sticks with a length of untwisted paper ribbon.

5. Twist the remainder of the untwisted paper ribbon around the bow and the cinnamon sticks in a random manner.

6. Fill the glass ball with potpourri and tie it to the end of the paper ribbon.

PEACH AND AQUA BASKET

A crescent design is used to accent the handle and front of this basket (see illustration on next page). Soft colors of peach and aqua are used. It is easily constructed by adding a few flowers to a pretty mesh bow. See color photograph on page 92.

You will need:

☐ One whitewashed peach basket, 12 inches (30.5 cm) wide × 12 inches (30.5 cm) tall × 5 inches (12.5 cm) deep

☐ 3 yards (2.7 m) 1¹/₂-inch-wide (4 cm) natural mesh ribbon

☐ Seven 1-inch (2.5 cm) peach rosebuds

Intermediate
1¹/₂ hours
$16 – $20

- ☐ Two 9-inch (22.5 cm) lengths silk ivy
- ☐ 3 yards (2.7 m) ¹/₂-inch-wide (1.3 cm) aqua satin picot-edged ribbon
- ☐ One eggshell chenille stem
- ☐ Sixteen ¹/₂-inch-wide (1.3 cm) aqua silk double-blossom flowers
- ☐ 30-gauge cloth-covered wire
- ☐ Glue

1. Form a ten-loop bow with the mesh ribbon as directed on page 16. Loops should measure 3 inches (7.5 cm) with two 18-inch (45.5 cm) streamers.

2. Secure the bow to the left side of the basket with the chenille stem. Curl the streamers around the handle, and glue the ends in place. Twirl the other streamer across the front of the basket and glue it in place.

3. Cut the aqua ribbon into nine 5-inch (12.5 cm) lengths. Form into nine single loops as directed on page 13. Glue the loops randomly between the loops of the mesh bow.

4. Cut the remaining aqua ribbon into two 18-inch (45.5 cm) lengths. Glue these streamers on top of the mesh ribbon streamers following the design in step 2.

5. Glue one ivy stem upward through the bow and one across the front of the basket.

6. Remove the roses from their stems and glue them in a crescent fashion through the bow loops and along the streamers.

7. Remove the aqua silk double blossoms from their stems, and glue them randomly to the looped streamers and between the bow loop.

BASKET WITH ASPARAGUS FERN

This would be a novel way to present a gift to a friend whose hobby is gardening. Fill it with gardening tools, seeds, a plant mister, and more! See color photograph on page 90.

Beginner
I hour
$15 – $17

You will need:

☐ One oval basket, 9 inches (22.5 cm) × 11 inches (28 cm) diameter × 13 inches (32.5 cm) tall × 4 inches (10 cm) deep

☐ 4-ounce package preserved asparagus fern

☐ Eighteen 1½-inch (4 cm) yellow silk flower blossoms

☐ 1-ounce bunch purple statice sinuata

☐ Glue

1. Cut the asparagus fern into 4-inch (10 cm) pieces. Glue in sections to

completely cover the edge of the basket. Glue a small cluster to the top center of the basket handle, also.

2. Remove the yellow blossoms from their stems. Glue them randomly into the asparagus fern around the basket edge and handle.

3. Break the purple statice into 1½-inch (4 cm) pieces. Randomly glue these into the asparagus fern between the yellow blossoms.

HEARTH BASKET

The rich jewel tones of the dried materials used on this basket coordinate beautifully with its elegant tapestry bow. Use it as a housewarming gift filled with a bottle of wine, pretty wine glasses, and cheese. See color photograph on page 94.

Intermediate
2 hours
$20 – $24

You will need:

☐ One oval willow basket, 11 inches (28 cm) × 15 inches (38 cm) diameter × 16 inches (40.5 cm) tall × 7 inches (17.5 cm) deep

☐ 2 yards (1.8 m) 2½-inch (6.5 cm) jewel-tone tapestry ribbon

☐ 4 ounces Spanish moss

☐ Twelve short peacock feathers

☐ Ten 1-inch (2.5 cm) dried yellow rosebuds

☐ 2-ounce package purple statice sinuata

- ☐ 2-ounce package natural baby's breath
- ☐ 2-ounce package green eucalyptus
- ☐ 2-ounce package peach cockscomb
- ☐ 2-ounce package preserved cedar
- ☐ Glue
- ☐ 30-gauge cloth-covered wire

1. Cut an 18-inch (45.5 cm) length of the tapestry ribbon. Make a V-cut into each end. Gather at the center with a 3-inch (7.5 cm) length of cloth-covered wire. Glue to the top center of the basket handle.

2. Make a four-loop tailored bow with the remaining tapestry ribbon as directed on page 20. The loops should measure 3 inches (7.5 cm) and 4 inches (10 cm). Glue these to the top center of the basket handle.

3. Glue a small amount of Spanish moss all around the rim of the basket.

4. Equally space the peacock feathers and dried yellow roses around the rim of the basket, and glue them into the moss.

5. Cut the rest of the dried materials to lengths of 2 inches (5 cm) to 3 inches (7.5 cm). Randomly glue these along the edge of the basket, filling in spaces between the roses and peacock feathers.

CHAPTER 9

Children's Designs

*W*himsical and colorful, the designs in this chapter will give you many ideas for creating bags, boxes, and baskets for children. Many are easy enough for children to do by themselves.

CLOWN BOX

Beginner
45 minutes
$10–$12

This gift box would make any child's eye sparkle with delight. The bright colors and clever design are just a hint of the goodies inside. See color photograph on page 93.

You will need:

- ☐ One red cardboard box, 6 inches (15 cm) square
- ☐ 1 1/2 yards (1.3 m) multicolored mum bow ribbon
- ☐ One brown chenille stem
- ☐ One 6-inch (15 cm) length of 3/4-inch-wide (1.8 cm) blue grosgrain ribbon
- ☐ One 18-inch (45.5 cm) length of 1 1/2-inch-wide (4 cm) rainbow stripe ribbon
- ☐ Two 1 1/4-inch (3.1 cm) gold premade package bows
- ☐ Two 3/4-inch (1.8 cm) oval movable eyes
- ☐ One blue party hat
- ☐ Glue
- ☐ One 1-inch (2.5 cm) black circle sticker

1. Cut an 18-inch (45.5 cm) length of mum bow ribbon. Pull the strings on each end to gather slightly. Glue this length along the top front edge of the box.
2. Cut two 3-inch (7.5 cm) lengths of chenille stems. Shape into eyebrows. Glue to the front of the box just below the mum bow ribbon.
3. Glue the gold bows under the eyebrows. Glue the eyes on top of the bows.
4. Glue the black sticker to the center of the box to represent a nose.
5. Glue the 6-inch (15 cm) length of grosgrain ribbon underneath the nose to form the mouth. Allow the ribbon to droop slightly to form the mouth.
6. Make a bow tie with the 18-inch (45.5 cm) length of rainbow ribbon, and glue it under the mouth.
7. Gather the remaining 1-yard (.9 m) length of the mum bow ribbon to form a large bow. Tie the ends together to secure. Glue this to the top right front corner of the box.
8. Attach a blue party hat to the top of the box.

NECKTIE BAG

Say, "Happy Father's Day" or "Happy Birthday, Dad" with this simply decorated bag. A tie would fit perfectly into this package. See color photograph on page 94.

Beginner
15 minutes
$2 – $5

Tie ribbons,
as shown, to
resemble
a necktie.

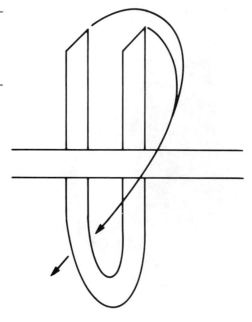

You will need:

☐ One striped gift bag, 4 inches (10 cm) × 14 inches (35 cm)

☐ 1 yard 1³/₈-inch-wide (3.4 cm) sheer copper wired ribbon

1. Cut a 10-inch (25.5 cm) length of ribbon. Tie across the width of the bag near the top. Position the knot to the back of the bag.

2. With the remaining ribbon, take the two ends together, slide them under the ribbon tied around the bag, and then place the ends through the loop at the opposite end of the length of ribbon (see diagram on next page). Pull tight.

3. Trim the ends of the ribbon to look like a necktie.

STICKER-DECORATED BAGS

Have you ever run out of wrapping paper? Check your children's sticker supply, and you're sure to find lots of wonderful items useful for decorating gift bags. This is also an easy way to let the children wrap their own presents for family and friends. See color photograph on page 93.

You will need:

☐ Assorted plain-colored gift bags or boxes or plain lunch bags

☐ Assorted stickers

Let kids use their imagination to design and decorate their own gift bags with self-adhesive stickers. They can add names, dates, or verses with crayons or markers.

Beginner
5 minutes!
$1 – $5

ANGEL BAG

This sweet angel gift bag would make a wonderful gift to give a child. It is simple enough for the child to create. See color photograph on page 93.

Beginner
30 minutes
$3 – $5

You will need:

☐ One colored lunch bag, 5 inches (12.5 cm) × 10 inches (25.5 cm)

☐ Two 8-inch (20 cm) white paper doilies

☐ One 6-inch (15 cm) white paper doily

☐ One 4-inch (10 cm) gold paper doily

☐ Pink construction paper

☐ Glue

☐ Stapler

☐ Black paint writer or marker

☐ 1/2 yard (.5 m) each of five different colors of 3/8-inch-wide (.9 cm) curling ribbon (total of 2 1/2 yards (2.3 m) of curling ribbon)

1. Place goodies in the bag.

2. Fold the 6-inch (15 cm) doily in half. Place it over the top of the bag. Fold the 4-inch (10 cm) gold doily in half, center it on top of the white doily. Staple the doilies to the bag. This forms the angel's collar.

137

3. Fold the two 8-inch (20 cm) doilies in half, then in quarters. Position them in between the folds at each side of the bag to form the angel's wings. Glue the front and back to secure.

4. Cut a 6-inch (15 cm) diameter circle from the pink construction paper for the face.

5. With the paint writer or marker, draw two eyes and a mouth. Allow to dry, then glue the face to the top of the bag.

6. Cut the curling ribbons into various lengths, 4 inches (10 cm) to 8 inches (20 cm) long. Curl the ribbons. Glue them to the top of the face to form the angel's hair.

SPONGE PAINTING

This type of painting is fun and easy for kids and adults. You can buy pre-cut sponges or cut your own design. See illustration below, and color photograph on page 93.

Beginner
10 minutes
$8 – $10

You will need:

☐ One canvas bag with handles, 4 inches (10 cm) × 6 inches (15 cm)

☐ 2¹/₂-inch (6.5 cm) tulip-shape sponge

☐ Bright pink fabric paint

☐ Green slick fabric paint

☐ Small fabric paintbrush

1. Apply the paint with a small brush to a damp sponge. Position the sponge on the surface to be painted. Press to apply the paint. Add as many tulips as you like. Allow to dry.

2. Squiggle green slick paint at the base of each tulip. Allow to dry.

CRAYON BASKET

Make a clever catch-all for loose crayons. Use new and used crayons to decorate the outside of this basket, along with some little felt figures. See color photograph on page 93.

Beginner
30 minutes
$6 – $10

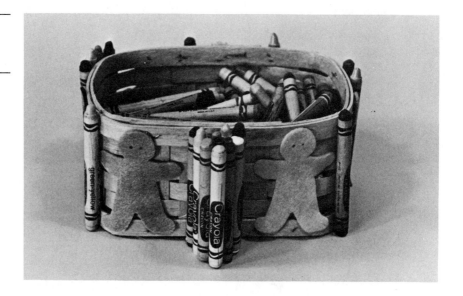

You will need:

☐ One oval basket, 4½ inches (11.3 cm) × 6½ inches (16.3 cm) diameter × 3 inches (7.5 cm) deep

☐ Six 3-inch (7.5 cm) felt figures (purchase these premade or cut your own from the pattern provided)

☐ Assorted crayons

☐ Glue

1. Glue two felt figures to the front and back of the basket. Center one felt figure to each side of the basket.

2. Glue clusters of crayons or single crayons randomly to the sides of the basket in between the felt figures.

Actual Size
to Cut
Gingerbread
Man

HAND PAINTING ON A LUNCH BAG

Make a rainy day fun with a little different version of finger painting. See color photograph on page 93.

Beginner
15 minutes
$1 – $3

You will need:

☐ One white paper bag, 6 inches (15 cm) × 12 inches (30.5 cm)
☐ Acrylic paints: red, blue, and yellow
☐ Small paintbrush
☐ Hands

1. Use the small brush to apply paint to hands.
2. Press hand on surface to be painted. Wash hands before applying a different color paint.

This is also a great technique to use on T-shirts or sweatshirt.

Index